DR. C. WALTER FERGUSON

LED TO THE STREAM

REFRESHING IN LIFE'S VALLEY

FOREWORD BY DR. CHARLES E. BOOTH

Copyright © 2018 by Dr. C. Walter Ferguson

Led to the Stream: Refreshing in Life's Valley
by Dr. C. Walter Ferguson

Printed in the United States of America

ISBN: 978-0-692-10014-1

All rights reserved. No part of this document may be reproduced or transmitted in any form, by any means (electronic, photocopying, recording, or otherwise) without the written permission of the author.

Unless otherwise indicated, Bible quotations are taken from the Holy Bible, English Standard Version. ESV® Text Edition: 2016. Copyright © 2001 by Crossway Bibles, a publishing ministry of Good News Publishers.

Scripture references marked "KJV" are from the King James Version of the Bible. Public domain.

Published by:
Gail Dudley, Highly Recommended Int'l Publishing

Cover by:
Jerrian Bell, KDC Marketing

Dedication

To my greatest motivators—Myrissa and C. J.
Thank you for reminding me
I am more than one thing.
I have finally risen above the fear of acceptance.
I am finally walking in uniqueness. I am all in!

To every reader—you are more than your journey.
Your journey is the enhancement to your next season.
Your valley has purpose.
Don't give up!
Don't quit!

TABLE OF CONTENTS

Foreword by Dr. Charles E. Booth vii

Introductory Thought
    A Job Circumstance with a Samson Chaser ix

Chapter 1
    A Cry for Help 17

Chapter 2
    Provision in a Dry Place 31

Chapter 3
    A Refresher Course in Praise 47

Chapter 4
    Don't Misinterpret My Struggle 59

Chapter 5
    The Value of the Process: Reaffirmed 73

Chapter 6
    The Value of the Process: Elevated 89

Chapter 7
    Overcoming Uncertainty 101
Chapter 8
    I Needed the Valley 115
Chapter 9
    Just When They Said It Was Over… 123
Final Thought
    Uncovering 135
About the Author 139

FOREWORD

It is not often that a pastor is offered the privilege of writing a foreword to a book penned by a son in the ministry. Such an honor is mine. I have known this author all of his life and what a joy it has been watching him mature into a Christian minister of immense gift and rich talent. Dr. C. Walter Ferguson has penned a work that needs to be read by those who occupy both pulpit and pew. *Led to the Stream: Refreshing in Life's Valley* is the product of this preacher's thoughtful insight about life's draining realities and one's need to find the refreshment that only the eternal can provide. One does not often come across such a work as this. Dr. Ferguson is one of those rare persons who can blend theology and life experience into a harmonious rhythm that reflects the joy/sorrow reality of the human experience. This preacher's journey into his own interior is a journey that reminds all of us of the path we, too, have traveled and continue to do so.

Blaise Pascal wrote in his work, *Pensées*, "The heart has reason the mind knows nothing about." Dr. Ferguson has unveiled his heart and allowed his mind to logically present issues that many would never allow this level of transparency to reach. We are very much in his debt for he travels a road that so many of us avoid.

I strongly recommend the reading of this work for in it one will get glimpses of one's own sojourn as one seeks the stream where the waters of rejuvenation await the thirsty pilgrim. As I read the pages of this work I was reminded of the words of Christian in *Pilgrim's Progress* when he says, "I have felt the bottom and it is secure." This, indeed, is the testimony of Dr. C. Walter Ferguson and all who shall read the thoughtful leaves of this author's virgin work.

Dr. Charles E. Booth, Pastor
Mt. Olivet Baptist Church
Columbus, Ohio
August 18, 2017

Introductory Thought

A Job Circumstance with a Samson Chaser

At the time of penning these thoughts, I find myself in an interesting period of time. I have entered my thirty-sixth year of living. In February of 2018, I celebrate twenty years of service to God in the preaching of the Gospel. I have seen five years of marriage and the continued growth of a mini me (more like a mini giant) named C. J. Family, friends, and familiar haunts surround me. Life is good…at least on the surface.

If I decided to leave this image as the backdrop of my existence, my participation in the enterprise of incomplete realities would be solidified. I'd rather take this platform to share with you a certain truth that is obvious, self-evident, and necessary. Our existence is greater and deeper than the superficial markers of success and contentment. As a matter of fact, many of us live in a world that promotes surface living rather than diving into the deep places of the heart, mind, and spirit. God has taken the time to remind me that we were not meant to be content with the minimum. We were designed to maximize our efforts to experience the totality of a truly abundant life (spirit, soul, mind, heart, etc.).

> **We were designed to maximize our efforts to experience the totality of a truly abundant life (spirit, soul, mind, heart, etc.).**

On our way to the experience of the abundant life we are guaranteed to encounter two prominent points—highs and lows. Consider this thought: People live for high moments. I listed many of the wonderful things and people that enhance my world. I acknowledged the milestones that are creating the texture of my path.

What was not emphasized were the lows. *Preacher, what could possibly bring you down?* Usually the response would begin with some type of qualification to prove my humanity, as if I have to tell any of you intelligent people that I am clay. However, the culture of status and position has conditioned many individuals to equate elite with absence of problems. We accept the rich, never addressing poor money management. We correlate disposable means, not strictly tangible, with the dismissal of mental health challenges.

The truth is I have, and still possess personal struggles. At different points in my journey, my manhood was questioned because I refused to live as a male chauvinist. My service in ministry has been judged by a social rubric created by individuals who do not value education, progress, and the leading of the Holy Spirit. I have not been the best covering for my wife socially, spiritually, or emotionally. I have battled clinical depression, isolation, low self-esteem, and social awkwardness. All of these aspects of my life left me facedown, weeping, repenting, and hopeless.

The interesting thing about life is that we need contrast. Challenges and conflict in our life develop our character and qualify our existence. The low places renew our appreciation for the high moments. Out of this reality is birthed the motivation to encourage people about valley navigation.

As we begin this journey, I must state a few ideas that will set the course for our journey.

1. Everyone will go to the valley.
2. God sends us to the valley for our good.
3. We can place ourselves in the valley for no beneficial purpose.
4. No one can stand on the mountain forever.
5. The valley is a necessary stop toward our destiny.

The valley of life is a place that can be most helpful to the follower of Jesus Christ. It can be a place of refreshing, renewal, and revival. The valley could become a place of self-loathing, suffering, and rehearsed martyrdom. The latter condition might occur if we fell off the mountain due to our missed steps or weakness.

The valley should not be strictly an instrument of correction or a low place that fosters our occasional sullen attitude. The valley is a place that God uses to refine our faith, strengthen our character, remove our self-centeredness, and restore our resolve. In this place, God takes us and creates the best form of ourselves.

At this moment, I feel like I am oversimplifying this environment, so allow me to inject two examples of valley navigators—Job and Samson. Many students of the Bible know the general level ideas of Job and Samson. Job was a righteous, family man who revered and worshipped God in every form possible (heart, soul, resources, etc.). Job interceded for his family on a daily basis. Job was internally and externally prosperous. You definitely could not beat his lifestyle. It was evident that God was blessing Job.

> **The valley is a place that God uses to refine our faith, strengthen our character, remove our self-centeredness, and restore our resolve.**

Job's life of blessings struck the ire of the devil. Satan challenged the legitimacy of Job's allegiance to God. That point of intellectual contention between God and the enemy birthed a challenge. Satan challenged the premise that Job's loyalty was rooted in the shallow dirt of the tangible. God placed the faith and character of Job before Satan and said in theory, "Take his stuff, his health, and his tangible prosperity. I know he won't bow down." Satan was hoping for humanity to hold to its selfish, superficial form. However, God knew the depth of Job's conviction and devotion.

Before we look at the results of the valley continuum, we must introduce the story of Samson. Unlike Job, Samson was set apart in the beginning of his life to do great things for God and Israel. Samson was a Nazarite from his birth. Along with the Law,

Samson needed to keep three aspects of this preordained vow.

1. Don't cut his locks.
2. Don't touch any dead thing.
3. Don't get drunk.

Simple enough, right? No big deal, right? This man was reckless in life, relationships, and service to God. Samson took for granted the supernatural strength associated with the obedience to the vow.

The insane reality of Samson's journey is God's grace was at work so many times before Samson took his trip to the valley. Consider this. The justice of God demanded satisfaction after Samson's drunken rage. However, God did not take away His power from Samson. Justice demanded retribution for Samson's unclean interaction with a honey-filled corpse. However, God's grace silenced the hounds. Romans 6 was not in the forefront of the mind of the power-lifting judge as he let a prostitute enter into his intimate space (emotional, physical, spiritual) in order to destroy him.

Examine this continuum. Two men from two different sets of issues arrive in the same valley. How is that possible? Remember, no one is exempt. The valley has a purpose. Any result of life can send us there. The result of this time must make people better to continue their journey of purpose.

Job lost money, children, health, and relationships. He was told that his sins brought him to this place. Job's wife became discontented with this alteration in lifestyle. She snapped by telling Job to curse God and die. Job began to question God and this situation. His friends became critics. Self-doubt became comfort for his sadness.

However, God spoke a word through a young man to put criticism at bay. Then God reminded Job of His reach, creativity, and power to restore abundant life. The process in the valley made Job a testament to faith under fire, endurance through struggle, and restoration after confrontation.

> **The process in the valley made Job a testament to faith under fire, endurance through struggle, and restoration after confrontation.**

Look at Samson. He arrives in the valley broken. His position broke him because he did not take the time to seek God. His relationships broke him because he sought fulfillment that only God provides. His anger made him abusive. His arrogance cost him physical sight. Samson's self-centeredness darkened the space for God's light. When all options left him, Samson regained his spiritual vision. He recognized that God's absence would take away his ability to fulfill his purpose.

At his lowest point, Samson repented of his apathy and pleaded for one more chance for destiny fulfillment. The judge conquered the Philistines by giving his life in one last act of power. Though he died, Samson's repentance lives as a testimony to how God repairs and restores.

On this continuum of valley entry, all of us will find a reason and a purpose for being present. However, our objective for the space of these written pages is discovering the various emotions, tools, and phases that will empower us to become stronger individuals, better leaders, committed disciples, and effective ambassadors of God.

May I share my prayer for this unfolding moment of literary travel? From my personal journey, I discovered many elements of my life that lingered without attention. My personal valley time stripped my preconceived notions about my own spirituality and theology. It brought me to the place of having no other options but the total Godhead. I have lost much for serving God the best way I knew how. However, I have gained over and above what tangibility provides. For that, I am grateful to my Father in Heaven.

Therefore, my prayer is that you receive what you need from this experience. I pray that on this literary excursion you will recognize that this path is not as lonely as you thought. The concept of *been there, done that,* may be more prevalent than you expected. As your brother in the faith, I pray that you will pass the blessings of this trip to others who need restoration. I pray that on the other side of the valley, you will be ready to climb again.

> **Our objective for the space of these written pages is discovering the various emotions, tools, and phases that will empower us to become stronger individuals, better leaders, committed disciples, and effective ambassadors of God.**

Let's begin…

Chapter 1

A Cry for Help

I lift up my eyes to the hills.
From where does my help come?
*My help comes from the L*ORD*,*
who made heaven and earth.
He will not let your foot be moved;
he who keeps you will not slumber.
Behold, he who keeps Israel
will neither slumber nor sleep.
*The L*ORD *is your keeper;*
*the L*ORD *is your shade on your right hand.*
The sun shall not strike you by day,
nor the moon by night.
*The L*ORD *will keep you from all evil;*
he will keep your life.
*The L*ORD *will keep*
your going out and your coming in
from this time forth and forevermore.
—Psalm 121

When you were a child, did you ever have a moment of fear? Did you ever get lost, and you thought no one would find you? Maybe you were stuck on a play set hoping you would not grow up with an apparatus as an extension of your being. Okay, maybe your fears were not sparked by those extremes.

Let's stay basic. Many people have a genuine fear of the darkness. Apparently, the absence of light causes emotions to stir in people. When darkness falls, people are forced to address feelings of the unknown, uncertainty, fright, and levels of paranoia generated by the horror film genre.

In the midst of darkness, we are challenged to respond in one of two ways—fight or flight. Most people are not willing to navigate through ominous circumstances willingly. Therefore, the instant response is the cry for help.

Help! The four-letter exclamation generates the faint hope that someone is capable of delivering us from problematic issues and unbearable burdens. Saying *help* attaches the expectation of rescue with understanding the reality of our personal limitations. The cry is one that ought to be a greater part of the human journey. However, most cries are ignored and unheeded by our society.

Consider for a moment our current social environment. We live in a world that is reverting back to many negative aspects of fifty years ago. Maligned groups are continuing to fight to be seen as human. Government officials are taking for granted the intellect of the electorate. Mental health issues are still seen as demonic issues and not medical concerns. The greedy are living on the sweat of the economically disenfranchised.

The cry for help has gone toward the tone-deaf ear of the world without an answer.

At this point, sermon discipline would incline the preacher to utter a shouting phrase—*But the Lord...* You fill in the blank. However, I can't help but imagine how many times we have glossed over the painful reality of being silenced by apathy. How many moments have come when someone looked at you and said, "You're being too emotional"?

Many places that ought to be infrastructures for emotional, intellectual, mental, and spiritual safety (local congregations, educational centers, etc.) have turned into platforms for exposing *weak faith*, lack of mental toughness, or emotional scattering. We must confess and repent of the incomplete theology of addressing pain and hurt. We must finally admit that the *fake it until you make it* teaching has failed us. We substituted the necessary process of healing and deliverance for a microwave option.

How many marriages could have been saved if we heard the genuine cries of the heart? How many relationships of all types could have avoided the signs of destruction if we paid attention? Minds have been fractured, souls confused, and spirits damaged for the sake of fostering an environment built on a shallow premise.

Consider also that we who attempt to lead in various institutions are not exempt from this painful theology. As much as we desire to create a safe place that people can work out their inner challenges, we are conditioned to the status quo. I acknowledge that many platforms that address helping or enhancing the environment of holistic life have people who are constantly exposed to burnout. Causes, people, and needs can drain the lifeblood of a servant. In many cases, safeguards are not always in place to aid the needs of leaders.

Martin Luther King, Jr. was known for battling depression and finding respite in hospital beds during seasons of great fatigue. Deified by the same nation that rejected the message of justice, King was a human being. Because of the truth he spoke, he was not approved by the masses. People wanted change, equality, and equity King advocated, but they could not handle the methodology or responsibility for carrying out the task of resistance. The weight of the struggle transferred to King and other vested leaders.

> **Many people never hear the pain, lament, or weariness of those who labor to carry out the vision and purpose of the Kingdom of God.**

As a pastor and ministry leader, I have witnessed the elation of the people when God worked in the life of the congregation. People are overjoyed with membership growth, communities taking notice of outreach, or other positive feedback. However, many people never hear the pain, lament, or weariness of those who labor to carry out the vision and purpose of the Kingdom of God. How many people have heard the following statements:

1. It's your job!
2. Why do we pay you so much?
3. You suck up to everyone.
4. Why are you at every event?
5. The Lord will work it out!

6. It ain't that serious!
7. Trust God and let it go!

These statements become so harmful and dangerous. The cries of servants, who want and need God to move in their lives, are stripped of the space to articulate their pain. These thoughts can potentially cripple the opportunity for healthy expression of trying moments and seasons.

I can speak to the segment of leadership I have represented for years. Some horrifying statistics exist about clergy burnout. I shared these stats with my previous congregation. Many of the older saints were horrified. The following statistics share the various concerns and elements of clergy burnout:

- 13% of active pastors are divorced.
- 23% have been fired or pressured to resign at least once.
- 25% don't know where to turn when they have a family or personal conflict or issue.
- 33% felt burned out within their first five years of ministry.
- 40% of pastors and 47% of spouses are suffering from burnout, frantic schedules, and/or unrealistic expectations.
- 45% of pastors' wives say the greatest danger to them and their family is physical, emotional, mental, and spiritual burnout.
- 45% of pastors say that they've experienced depression or burnout to the extent that they needed to take a leave of absence from ministry.
- 50% feel unable to meet the needs of the job.

- 32% of pastors say they and their spouses believe that being in pastoral ministry is hazardous to their family's well-being and health.
- 56% of pastors' wives say that they have no close friends.
- 57% would leave the pastorate if they had somewhere else to go or some other vocation they could do.
- 70% don't have any close friends.
- 75% report severe stress causing anguish, worry, bewilderment, anger, depression, fear, and alienation.
- 80% of pastors say they have insufficient time with their spouse.
- 80% believe that pastoral ministry affects their families negatively.
- 90% feel unqualified or poorly prepared for ministry.
- 90% work more than 50 hours per week.
- 94% feel under pressure to have a perfect family.
- 1,500 pastors leave their ministries each month due to burnout, conflict, or moral failure (featured on pastorburnout.com).[1]

Scary, right? Spiritual leaders are admitting to be flesh and blood. Human beings with great responsibilities are confessing that their frail humanity cannot bear the weight of the cross. Though these stats place a male context to the pastorate, women who occupy

---

[1] "Pastor Burnout Statistics," *PastorBurnout.com*., http://www.pastorburnout.com/pastor-burnout-statistics.html.

the role of undershepherd invariably face the same challenges. In a more general sense, pain, suffering, and burnout are not reserved for any one group. Therefore, the need for refreshing is necessary for everyone who is dry and thirsty.

I write this labor of love at a time when each of these statistics has rung true in my life. I am a relatively young man who has experienced many things. I am a husband, father, and servant of God. Honesty compels me to share that it has been a difficult journey trying to live to God's standard while being told that I am nothing but a failure. *What do you mean, preacher?*

Imagine being well schooled in theology, married to a powerful woman of God, and having the cutest little boy ever (yes, I'm biased) but to be told that we don't want all of you. We want your preaching acumen and youth, but don't tell us that women, including your wife (an ordained preacher), can be used by God. We want the potential for a huge congregation, but we don't want to walk with you.

That feeling may be horrible, but my reaction was worse. I attempted to deny the divine spark God placed in me. I suppressed my creativity, vision, and purpose in the name of unity. At the same time, denying who I was caused me to try and hold my family under the same bondage. Why? I needed to put food on the table. Ha! I tried to sell out. What harm could it do?

A denial of God's creative excellence resulted in multiple hospital ER visits, marriage strain, financial hardship, clinical depression, a miscarriage of our second child, isolation, obesity, and self-doubt. Psalm 139:14 did not ring true in this season of my life:

I praise you, for I am fearfully and wonderfully made.
Wonderful are your works; my soul knows it very well.

It was not *well with my soul*. My family shed many tears that I could not dry. I shed tears nobody could or wanted to dry away. I shed tears that only God could take away. However, I felt unworthy of that help.

Maybe I am speaking to your situation right now. Before we press toward the answer, it might be the right moment to acknowledge the pain. Recognize the suffering that has permeated your environment. However (here's the shouting moment), God loves us beyond our current condition and is ready to help us. Nothing can separate us from His love (Romans 8:31-39). The Lord is ready to help us only if we look to Him.

So God is ready to help us? Wonderful! Are we ready to receive the help? Possibly. Let us address this reality with a guiding question. Why must we look to God in these trying seasons of life? Allow me to offer at least three ideas for your consideration.

Taking Our Minds Off of Our Valley Struggle

When we enter into Psalm 121, we discover a song that leads us on a journey toward a destination. Along the way, the writer grants us a poetic cry of help to make it through the journey. This traveling image grants us a perspective of looking toward an elevated plane. By default, the journeyman is in a valley-like condition.

As the poem continues, we are given the insight that all of the traveler's confidence rests in God. The Lord would preserve in all conditions. God is concerned about the well-being of those who seek after Him. God is aware and intimately acquainted with the turnstile known as our lives. That reality brought peace and tranquility to this psalmist.

In the journey of life, we are constantly attempting to figure out the next move; who is on our side; why are we in this predicament. The consumption of our brain matter dealing with these issues can magnify our discontentment with our circumstances.

When we face challenges, it is a lonely feeling. We may say to ourselves, *Nobody cares* or *Why did they leave?* We run through a list of deserters, complications, issues, or difficulties that plague our existence. However, we never take the time to consider the presence, power, and love of God.

> **The fact that God keeps His promises should ignite a deep sense of hope when we are facing internal or external strife.**

An interesting thing about the Creator; we are promised not to be forsaken by Him. His presence is so vast that we are told no matter where we are, He is there. God is never short of His Word. The fact that God keeps His promises should ignite a deep sense of hope when we are facing internal or external strife.

One of the greatest joys of my life is being a father. Many of my friends have been blessed to have contact or amazing relationships with their fathers. I was never blessed or fortunate to have my father's care or presence. I will confess, that is a driving force for me to be active in Charles Jeremiah's life.

CJ has known my voice from the time he was in Myrissa's womb. Every night, I talked to him as he was developing. I did not do that baby talk nonsense. *(Sidenote: Talk to your kids like human beings. They do understand.)* I told CJ my plans and goals as a father. I told him my dreams for his life. I figured he knew my voice.

July 11, 2014. Charles Jeremiah Ferguson was born. As the doctor showed me my mini me, I felt overwhelmed. However, the next moment changed my perspective on life. The nurses began running tests, doing hand and footprints, and checking vitals. I was watching from a distance when I heard my little man crying. The physician looked at me and saw the jitters of a first-time dad. "It's okay. Go see your son," she said.

> **Our difficult places are not permanent. They are points along the journey that remind us we can make it.**

I walked over and looked over his little body while he cried at all his newfound attention. "Hey little man. Daddy's here," I uttered. Suddenly, cries morphed into a deep sigh of relief. He shed not another tear. Not one more cry was uttered. He knew Daddy was present.

The knowledge of God's presence can produce two responses. First, we can feel peace. It is not the absence of trouble. Peace is the state of tranquility in the midst of evident chaos. Peace is the condition of knowing that everything will come together regardless of circumstances (Romans 8:28).

When God is present, we are able to look at difficulty with a renewed spirit. Trouble on your job is no longer a distraction. Conflict with family becomes an opportunity to heal deep wounds. Personality irritation develops into moments of introspection. God grants us the space to be vulnerable while developing the strategy for our deliverance.

Secondly, we gain determination. God as Emanuel in our existence grants us the hope to make it through the challenge. Our difficult places are not permanent. They are points along the journey that remind us we can make it. At every stage God will walk with us and remind us that He cares about everything. With confidence we can declare that we feel like going on.

REMEMBER GOD IS IN CONTROL

When addressing internal, external, emotional, or spiritual chaos, it can be difficult trying to find a way to see the hand of God at work. Truthfully, most people suggest that they cannot recognize the tapestry being crafted by God. We can't see the loose strings behind it or appreciate the complete work seen by the world. Why? We are preoccupied with our challenges and current condition.

The concept of control for any human being is a serious challenge. We are accustomed to having the ability to manipulate or alter issues or situations to be favorable. What happens when the option of control is taken away?

Job was a faithful man. Job feared God. Job embraced worshipping God. Yet, Job lost everything in the natural realm of value and significance. Job could not regrow crops, regain land, or procreate during this season because his health would not permit, his mind could not conceive the suffering, and his wife disconnected from him. In spite of all of this difficulty, God is the author and finisher of our faith. God encompasses every aspect of our living.

Yet, the key to this experience rests in our yielding to God. Second Chronicles 7:14 reminds us of three attributes to experiencing God's control over our situation—humility, active relationship (seeking His face), and repentance (turn from our wicked ways). We must be humble or humbled to recognize our method and process of survival and prosperity is incomplete without the Lord.

> **We must be humble or humbled to recognize our method and process of survival and prosperity is incomplete without the Lord.**

To declare unto God and the world, "I put it all in His hands," is the greatest act of submission one can make. It marks complete trust and dependency on God to handle the strategy, planning, and ultimate deliverance from my situation. God will not allow weapons of mass destruction to triumph in your life (Isaiah 54:17). God will keep you at all times (Matthew 28:20). God will not allow anything to separate us from His presence (Romans 8:30-39).

FIND PEACE IN HIS PROTECTION

The Lord keeps, protects, shades, and preserves. The psalmist makes the claim. The Lord is concerned about the totality of our being. What better gift in life than to have the Creator of the universe provide peace of mind concerning you? In other words, trouble or disappointment comes for you. Put it in His hands. We don't have Blessed Assurance alone when God is involved. However, He provides Blessed Insurance for our purpose, future, and destiny.

The apostle Paul reminds us, "do not be anxious about anything, but in everything by prayer and supplication with thanksgiving, let your requests be made known to God. And the peace of God, which surpasses all understanding, will guard your hearts and minds in Christ Jesus" (Philippians 4:6-7).

Through our avenues of relationship—prayer, worship, and meditation—we rediscover the power of God's peace. We don't have to consume our energy in trying to find solutions. We don't need to dedicate our total mental, emotional, and spiritual capital to distracting agendas. We can find peace in knowing that God is the originator of the Olivia Pope theology displayed on the television show, *Scandal*: "It's handled."

While we are in our life-altering season, we must take the time to be reintroduced to God. Many of us know God according to our initial introduction. However, we must learn new aspects of His glory and presence. Specifically, our weeping is an opportunity to watch Him dry our tears. Embrace this moment. God is ready to answer your cry for help.

Chapter 2

Provision in a Dry Place

But he himself went a day's journey into the wilderness and came and sat down under a broom tree. And he asked that he might die, saying, "It is enough; now, O Lord, take away my life, for I am no better than my fathers." And he lay down and slept under a broom tree. And behold, an angel touched him and said to him, "Arise and eat." And he looked, and behold, there was at his head a cake baked on hot stones and a jar of water. And he ate and drank and lay down again. And the angel of the Lord came again a second time and touched him and said, "Arise and eat, for the journey is too great for you." And he arose and ate and drank, and went in the strength of that food forty days and forty nights to Horeb, the mount of God.
—1 Kings 19:4-8

Have you ever traveled to a really warm climate? (It doesn't have to be the Caribbean specifically. Don't brag!) Have you ventured to a location that air conditioning was a greater commodity than food? I am born and bred a Buckeye (native of Ohio) who grew up in a weather climate that was guaranteed to grant your every seasonal desire in a short period of time. My background should have prepared me for any type of weather craziness. I have been wrong on more than one occasion.

During my master of divinity work, I had a requirement to take part in a crosscultural immersion experience. It was an exciting and amazing opportunity. However, I was positioned to choose a trip that was closer to home. See, I had just begun my first pastorate in Circleville, OH at the Second Baptist Church. I figured being a new pastor meant that going overseas was out of the question.

I decided to take my pilgrimage through the beautiful areas of Arizona and New Mexico. What an unbelievable experience. What a life-changing moment. I met God at monasteries, the mountains, and the capital of the Indian Nation. I had flashbacks to my Kentucky State University days when I visited Diné College in Tsaile, AZ. The great sense of Navajo pride ignited my memory of my black college experience. My spirit and soul connected with my great grandfather, Rev. Frank J. Winbush, while walking in many of the places he saw.

This fulfilling experience was almost overshadowed by the end of a three-mile hike. Arizona and New Mexico house two major environmental attributes—mountainous elevations and dry desert places. What a combination. You have to address lower oxygen levels or dry heat at any given moment. On this day, the dry heat defeated me.

I did not take into consideration how much I needed to focus on my hydration. I didn't feel sweaty. It was 90 degrees, but it was not unbearable. I was not tired like in the days of football two-a-days. I really believed that I was fine.

We caravanned in our vehicles down the road as we were leaving our hiking site. We were preparing to make a stop to get a bite. Suddenly, I found myself doubled over dry heaving on the side of the road. I tried to pull it together. I told myself that I was okay. My body did not agree. I ended up confined to a bed at a monastery for two days. I couldn't move. I couldn't function. I was the victim of dry conditions.

We live our lives under changing mental, emotional, and spiritual conditions. Some days we are flowing in the peace and joy of God. We feel almost untouchable by the conditions of life. Other days come when we are so overwhelmed that the life force within our being is sucked dry. The difficulties and issues of our environment parch us.

These unforeseen moments cause us to discover our positioning during our figurative heatstroke in a desert place. We are pushed and frustrated by the prospect of surviving in such a place without supplies for renewal. In this space, the promise of God to supply every need is challenged fiercely.

Think about your greatest moments of being parched. Your dry season may have come after a great personal victory. You gave your mental energy, emotional stock, and spiritual investment toward conquering a major hurdle. When the shouting ends, reality sets in quickly. Life has not ended. Challenges continue to come our way. But, are we ready? Can we recharge in the desert moments of life?

Let us ponder on the subject of 1 Kings 19—Elijah. The prophet is a powerful object lesson for many leaders, religious or otherwise. Elijah was a bold prophet that spoke out against the mishandling of God's earthly kingdom, Israel. Elijah watched as Ahab and Jezebel swayed the nation toward greater idol worship and practice.

Interestingly enough, the corrupted crown leaned on the ear itching, propheticless (yes, I made it up) word of the messengers of Baal. They placed their dependency and values in the hands of a tangible god that was not spiritually accessible to the people. What a mess to live in. Sounds like a nation that I know too well.

Station Break moment:

Regardless of your political ideologies, one thing is consistent for me. We live in a nation in need of more God-inspired, Holy Spirit driven, anointed prophetic voices in the United States. We became...excuse me...we have always been a country that places our hopes, ambitions, and aspirations in the frail hands of biased social structures and greedy self-serving interests.

We are in need of God's chosen to speak truth to power. We need voices that will tell Pharaoh that he is wrong. We need voices that will not silence God by making Him a platform. We need people who will speak empowerment to the disenfranchised and hope to the hopeless. The task is great, but the work is necessary.

The work of Elijah becomes a great witness and tragic story when looking through the lens of change and justice. Elijah challenges 450 prophets of Baal to see who served the true and living God. A demonstration of Yahweh's power proved that Baal was at best a flawed concept. Elijah had the prophets killed. Victory was captured. The name of the Lord was magnified.

Elijah should be walking tall after such an experience. However, Jezebel sent a decree announcing her intentions to kill Elijah. The "prophet" R. Kelly was right when he declared, "When a woman's fed up, there ain't nothing you can do about it." Something about Jezebel's anger set off a pocket of fear within Elijah. The idea of revenge killing set off serious depression within the prophet. How can someone end up in such a depleted place after witnessing such a demonstration of power?

May I submit to you that the energy that is necessary to walk and function in the anointing of God covers many of our fatal flaws from public view. Many great orators have the fear of crowds. Great athletes are afraid to fail. Many believers do not want to disappoint God. Nobody wants to be exposed as weak.

Our current environmental construct makes people experience personal anxiety. The inner conflict is understood as a sign of spiritual ineptitude or weakness. The truth is we are seeking outlets to gain the refreshing we seek from God. Yes, I hear you, great saints! Our relationship with God grants us twenty-four-hour access to what we need. We agree.

Nevertheless, our dryness can challenge our will to seek closely the presence of God. Let's just say it. The Lord we love, the Creator of the ends of the earth, Alpha and Omega, and so on is not always our first choice. We will choose a cactus (a miserable friend, controlled substance, friends with benefits, debt) to grant satisfaction because we do not explicitly see our source of Living Water.

Elijah ran to the wilderness not to seek God, but he sought for his own personal demise. He was not seeking reassurance from God. Elijah was looking for a speedy release from his misery. *Take my life…it is enough*. What a statement of internal turmoil. Yet, God took this moment of crisis to demonstrate He could be found anywhere.

We can only imagine or assume how quickly God would have moved for Elijah if the circumstances focused squarely on God's saving power. What would have occurred if Elijah ran to a prayer partner, another God-fearing prophet, or a remnant that would not bow to the idol? We will not know.

However, we can be certain that positive seeking of God can render almost immediate results. The negative state of Elijah called to the heart and mission of God. Jehovah decided to use the relationship with Elijah as an opportunity to show the prophet that His reach and provision can meet him in a dry place and restore his soul for the next move in his life.

The Scripture acknowledges a few elements that we cannot ignore for our journey through understanding provision in dry spaces:

1. God provides regardless of condition.
2. Provision and relationship are not mutually exclusive.
3. Provision has a purpose.
4. We need provision to continue.
5. God's provision will carry us beyond our limitations.

The key to pressing on comes back to the foundation of relationship. Our relationship taps into resources in hard times. Relationship unveils the path we must take to fulfill our purpose.

When Jesus left the earth, He gave a command, a purpose, and a promise in the midst of the dryness the disciples were experiencing:

> *Go therefore and make disciples of all nations, baptizing them in the name of the Father, and of the Son, and of the Holy Spirit, teaching them to observe all that I have commanded you. And behold, I am with you always to the end of the age.*
> —Matthew 28:19-20

Jesus made it a point to remind the disciples and us that the conditions and environment do not change the reality of His presence and our mission. He promises to go with us through the roller coasters of life that we might fulfill our destiny and live a complete life.

We are confident that God will provide. We are resolved that circumstances do not alter His promise, so we must take a moment to unearth the specific provisions that we receive in the desert of life.

A Reminder of God's Approval

Recall our Scripture and focal subject for a moment. Elijah was victorious over the 450 prophets of Baal. However, Jezebel was trying to impose deadly consequences and repercussions. The attacks on Elijah's psyche sent him into a deep depression. He wrote himself off regarding how God should see him.

God made a profound decision to demonstrate His love and approval of Elijah in the greatest way possible. The Lord fed him. It is one thing for Bobby Flay, G. Garvin, Sunny Anderson, or Emeril Lagasse to prepare a plate, but God will lay a table out for you if you let Him.

The magnitude of feeding Elijah extends beyond our view of addressing hunger. God did not accept the demands of the prophet, because God knew how valuable Elijah was. God recognized the real hunger that rested in Elijah at that moment—affirmation. I hear my professors and mentors attempting to call me to task on the potential imposition of an idea. Bear with me.

The relationship between God and Elijah was based in trust, love, and honor. Elijah's love for God was expressed through his worship, living, and preaching. Elijah trusted God because of the Almighty's track record of fulfilled promises and tasks regardless of opposition. The prophet honored God by committing his life to the Kingdom cause. He laid everything down for the purpose of giving God his best. At this moment, Elijah is tapped out. His reserve is nonexistent. He has nothing more to give anyone.

The love, trust, and honor Elijah attempts to demonstrate through human frailty are magnified by the same attributes being shown by God. Jehovah loved Elijah. He knew that in this deep place of hopelessness Elijah needed something to validate his existence. God honored Elijah by meeting the prophet's need. God reaffirmed his trust in Elijah by intentionally strengthening his servant for the journey.

Humanity is in constant need of affirmation. We should not live for it. It should not be the focus of our every pursuit in life. However, affirmation applied to our lives yields a healthy dose of encouragement and strength to exhibit our authentic selves.

I was blessed and honored to serve as the senior pastor of a church in Springfield, IL. During my short time, I experienced many of the ups and downs that can plague pastors from time to time. I will forever be grateful for the victories seen and the people who lifted my arms while pursuing my purpose and call in that branch of Zion.

At one point of my service, I was dealing with a serious moment of oppression concerning my call, uniqueness, and purpose.

> **Affirmation applied to our lives yields a healthy dose of encouragement and strength to exhibit our authentic selves.**

A select, loud few decided that my gift was a great asset, but it was not living or functioning in the proper, desired package. It hurt. The constant pressing was painful. The shadow of depression was closing in fast. My routine suffered. My office was no longer a place of solace. Anger and discouragement allowed me to commiserate over my circumstances. I lamented over my fleeting authenticity.

One day in the office, I found myself in another wrestling match with my emotions. I just could not get my day moving at all. My lungs proved to be in great shape while I looked over my Bible and study notes. My despair was great. My heart was grieved. It was at the lowest moment possible I heard a knock at my door. God sent an angel by my way. Her name is Sister Jackie.

Sister Jackie is maybe a little bit over five feet tall. She has a passion and a desire for the Kingdom of God. She is also no nonsense about respect for the pastor. I am totally convinced that Sister Jackie was among many whom I knew for sure prayed for my family and me every day. So, her presence in the office was not only welcomed, but it was a pleasant surprise.

"Pastor," she said, "I was thinking about you over the past week. I kept saying that I was going to get over to the church, but things kept happening." I figure she had Jesus on speed dial. If I ever needed someone to speak to my heart an unusual amount of encouragement, I was in deep need at that very moment. She continued, "I didn't come to talk about me. I just wanted to check on you and see if you are okay. I noticed that you haven't been yourself lately." As my eyes well with tears recalling this conversation, the same water streamed down my cheeks as she spoke that simple sentiment.

The complete conversation does not have a transcript for sharing with the world. However, something must be understood. God grants us beautiful moments that we must not always divulge to the world. God gives us gifts that are specific for us. Yet, I can share that this encounter with Sister Jackie was bread from heaven for my hungry soul.

In that moment, God reminded me that it was fine to be a vessel that was sensitive to the movement of the Holy Spirit. It is okay to care for your family in every manner possible. I was not weak for making my wife and child a priority (see 1 Timothy 3). Teaching and preaching the Bible is right and proper. I was tired of being told that traditional was holiness. The manner that God crafted me was not only good enough, but it was exactly what was necessary for the advancement of the Lord's vision.

Everyone ought to have some *bread* that God sends to feed your spirit. Our egos are not in need. Our spirit needs the moment to actually reflect on the creative genius of God. We did not create our existence. Yet, God thought enough about our design to make us useful, powerful, and impactful to our environment. It is the gift of knowing it was *He who made us, and we are His; we are His people, and the sheep of His pasture* (Psalm 100:3).

> **The affirmation of the Creator of the universe carries greater weight than the vitriol and hatred that people can spew in our direction.**

Knowing that you are loved and embraced by God begins the rebuilding process of our inner being. The affirmation of the Creator of the universe carries greater weight than the vitriol and hatred that people can spew in our direction. Affirming your sacred existence is necessary.

Confidence to Not Second-Guess Yourself

The threat of the queen drew a response within Elijah that was contrary to his recent stand against 450 misguided souls. Could it be that Elijah thought that repentance would have come after the demonstration of God's power? Is it possible that disappointment came upon this mouthpiece because the visible activity of God did not move the leaders that needed the reminder of who Jehovah was?

These questions are not explicit. The implication may not be traced. But, the human side of our witness can call into question the moments when God did not meet our expectations. Yes, brothers and sisters, we have expectations of God that are heavily rooted in our limited perspective. It is laughable that we could ever imagine the Lord having to meet a set of completed work criteria set by us; but we try it all the time.

Imagine the other part of Elijah's mind at the time. I imagine the thoughts of the prophet sounding something like this: "You mean to tell me that they weren't changing after fire? Fire! What type of stuff is this? I put my life on the line, because I believe in you. You know what? Let me just die. I might as well. There's no help for me in Israel. I'm a dead man anyhow."

Even when the Spirit of God moves upon us, we might encounter a moment when the results do not match the magnitude of the movement. Was it your fault? No. Was it God's fault? No. Was it lack of prayer, reading, meditation, or fasting? Nope. The simple truth is that all will not receive the truth.

Preachers are notorious for this thought pattern: "Nobody shouted, danced, or fell out over this sermonic exercise. God must have left us behind. You know what? If I could whoop like E. Dewey Smith, exegete like Charles E. Booth, or articulate like Gardner Taylor, I could finally preach." Apparently preaching the truth is not enough. We begin to second-guess our purpose.

It is not for us to know how God is going to work the movement of His Spirit. As a matter of fact, I need to tell every believer, young preacher, or leader a simple truth. God does not function according to formulas. He moves as He pleases. God manifests His presence according to His desire.

Young preacher, baby brother, baby sister, listen to me. All responses are not evidence of God's will being performed. Every shout is not confirmation of understanding. Every contemplative face is not judgmental or cold. Every church will not equip you with a good organ bump. But, God has given you the Word, mission, and Holy Spirit necessary to speak truth to power.

> **When things don't happen like we hoped, it is an opportunity for God to reveal the bigger picture in relationship to our past victory or Kingdom activity.**

When things don't happen like we hoped, it is an opportunity for God to reveal the bigger picture in relationship to our past victory or Kingdom activity. Defeating the 450 prophets of Baal was only the wick attached to the C-4 God was preparing to release in the world. Elijah was not aware of the holy coalition that was forming to set Israel in place again (see 1 Kings 19:14-18). When doubt attempts to enter in our minds, we must remember our journey has usefulness beyond this acute stage.

COURAGE TO MOVE FORWARD

In the desert God cared for Elijah. God fed the prophet, but take notice of a subtle nuance. Elijah was fed for two consecutive days. On the second day of food delivery, the weary man was commanded to eat because *the journey was too great*. Do not gloss over this statement. Jehovah Jireh provided with intent. It was time for Elijah to rise from his place to his next destination.

The provision of God gave a broken man the energy to move forward. Notice the writer does not indicate resistance by Elijah to travel forward. The Scripture says that after Elijah ate he left for Horeb—a forty-day journey. What kind of supernatural flour was used in that cake? Forty days? That thought is not the important point. Recognize that all of Elijah's issues were not yet fixed; but he moved forward.

Brothers and sisters, some of you may not realize how challenging it is to move one step forward from the painful places of life. For many people, the issues of mental and emotional health have been so taboo in the world and the church. The very nature of pressing forward one step at a time is so significant.

I have shared from the pulpit on different occasions my battles with suicidal tendencies as a young man. Yes, I grew up in the church with great preaching and teaching surrounding me. I knew that God was able. However, low self-esteem was my struggle. I was picked on by many of my peers. I was the fat kid, the nerd, and the *white-talking* boy. I was worthless.

Many people that have known me for years may read this work for the first time and have reactions of shock, disbelief, judgment, or a dismissive attitude. I want you to understand it has taken many tears, days, conversations, and prayers to arrive at the place of openness and vulnerability. My declaration is like many who have been maligned and marked as ones who lack faith. I thank God that my plans to end it all never prospered. I am grateful that God knew my worth and never counted me out.

I plead with your spirit now to recognize how powerful a moment it is when one can declare, "I am in pain, but I won't quit. I can't give up until I'm whole. This place is not the end of my story." God knew that restoration was needed. He knew Elijah was dry, but he was in the right condition for deliverance from inner turmoil. When you are facing dry seasons, remember the penned words of Horatio Palmer:

To him that o'er cometh, God giveth a crown,
Through faith we will conquer, though often cast down;
He who is our Savior, our strength will renew;
Look ever to Jesus, He'll carry you through.

Ask the Savior to help you,
Comfort, strengthen, and keep you;
He is willing to aid you,
He will carry you through.[2]

---

[2] Horatio Palmer, "Yield Not to Temptation," *Hymnary.org*, https://hymnary.org/hymn/NNBH1977/188.

Chapter 3

A Refresher Course in Praise

> *Make a joyful noise to the* LORD, *all the earth!*
> *Serve the* LORD *with gladness!*
> *Come into his presence with singing!*
> *Know that the* LORD, *he is God!*
> *It is he who made us, and we are his;*
> *we are his people, and the sheep of his pasture.*
> *Enter his gates with thanksgiving,*
> *and his courts with praise!*
> *Give thanks to him; bless his name!*
> *For the* LORD *is good;*
> *his steadfast love endures forever,*
> *and his faithfulness to all generations.*
> —Psalm 100

How smart are you? No, I mean it. I want you to think about your assessment of your intelligence. Are you average? Above average? MENSA worthy? I figure that everyone reading this book is more intelligent than I am. I have multiple degrees and mounds of student loans (that I will conquer). You, dear brother and sister, are the bright ones.

I begin with a little self-indicting humor because many times we read books that have great, profound meaning, but we do not give ourselves the opportunity to breathe and reassess our journey. This literary exercise is not just for an ego trip or your amusement. My hope is that through this cathartic and revelatory release you will experience a state of hope and renewal. If nothing else, my prayer is that this piece would be a refresher course in addressing the ebb and flow of life.

Every person I know needs a time to unlearn, relearn, or equip him- or herself for new challenges. Many employers place an emphasis on continued training. Most major companies have academic reimbursement programs designed to encourage education enhancement for employees. President Barack H. Obama traveled around the country to champion the cause of community colleges as an integral part of the revitalization of the American workforce.

The debate continues in our nation about having a choice regarding private or public school education models. On either side of the debate, a myriad of issues are taking away from one inexplicable premise. Education must be a constantly evolving aspect of life. The uneducated individual is subject to harming the environment they inhabit. His or her willing ignorance will not enhance growth, but perpetuate tolerance for the status quo.

We must also consider it wisdom to place ourselves in a position to be an eternal learner. By becoming long-term students, we are given the opportunity to gather new methods and concepts regarding previously obtained knowledge. We begin to refashion our scope regarding everything. From culture to science, we rediscover our love for various subject matters, renewal of our commitment to excellence, and revival of our desire for participation. So I ask again. How smart are you?

When we find ourselves in the valley of life, we may not consider it a moment to praise God initially. I submit to you a thought for your consideration. Everything about being on top of the world is not beautiful. In a later chapter, I will lay out the complete necessity for the valley. However, we must understand for the sake of this idea that the mountaintop experience we seek exposes us to the clear attack of the wicked.

Therefore, entering into the valley at certain moments should grant us pause to praise God for His protection from dangers seen and unseen. Many times, we are on top of the world and the thin air affects our memory. We did not gain victory on our own. (Now enter your shouting cue.) If it had not been for the Lord on our side, tell me, where would we be?

We don't want to admit it. We don't want to confess it. Our praise is influenced more by our condition than our God. The impetus of our praise should be the One who delivered our lives from a burning literal and figurative hell. Every congregation assembled as a group of baptized believers should have moments every Sunday where introverts and extroverts find themselves in uninhibited awe of God.

Unfortunately, every church is not subject to that reality. Let's be honest. Many churches do studies, surveys, and institutional research in order to reach one conclusion—the biblical prescription for praise is still undefeated. How that concept comes forth will be debated ad nauseam. But, the Bible is still right.

Sometimes we don't have to reinvent the wheel. We need to reexamine the foundation for deeper revelation. Upon a new, fresh look, God will reveal what is necessary for us to do in this season of spiritual growth. Let us take a look at a familiar place in Scripture.

Psalm 100 is a selection in a group of "elementary Scriptures" that most churchgoers learned in the infancy of their walk with God. The writer is determined to express to us the deep adoration that is experienced in serving the Lord. The song is one that invites us to glean the moments of one worshipping the Almighty God.

Our examination of the text reveals many elements to the praise and worship oozing from the lyrics. We are implored to do the following:

1. Shout.
2. Serve with gladness.
3. Sing Acknowledging the Lofty Place of God.
4. Recognize God's creativity.
5. Publicly praise God.
6. Embrace His eternal greatness.

That list might appear long, but measure it against His works in our lives. It is the least we can do. Our engagement with these commands is a sign of our willingness to be open with our relationship with God.

The nature of our relationship is extremely paramount in our Christian walk. It is the difference between religion and spiritual connection. Relationship with God takes the guesswork out of achieving religion. Relationship causes us to engage God because of love, trust, and genuine interest. Religion places the weight of legalism as the measurement of God's desire concerning us.

On the other side, I can understand why people love religion. It takes away the emotional and spiritual attachment to God. If we follow a set of rules and regulations, we will gain the reward of a pious existence. If we mess up, we will face the consequences and maybe do better next time. Religion does not leave room to break God's heart. Religion does not offer a space to feel sadness or misery of disappointing God. Simply put, we get all we want or need without the mess.

Maybe the messiness of relationship is our problem as human beings. Humanity was created to be in relationship. God made us in His image and likeness. We were the only creation that was handcrafted and given the essence of God that made us a living soul. Plus, Adam and Eve were granted daily walking access with God. But, the mess became Humanity choosing sin over God while living in a perfect world. Adam and Eve got kicked out. Yet, God so loved the world that He gave…you know the rest.

Love can have painful moments. Love has redeeming traits. That reality is why Hollywood writes the movies that beacon me to a minimum of two hours of a romantic comedy while sitting on a sofa with my wife. The uncertain moments that arise in relationship with God can challenge our understanding of Him. It can push us to declare His goodness from the rooftop.

Either way, the excitement of the roller coaster with God yields more fulfillment and real interaction than stagnation of a business transaction. The psalmist is pushing us to refresh our minds to recognize the best and beneficial steps in experiencing powerful and redeeming praise.

The Joy in Knowing God

The psalmist writes, "Make a joyful noise unto the Lord." Joy is a condition that is not influenced by the circumstances of the external. It is predicated on the inner workings of the one who is connected to God. No matter what people may do, situations may dictate, or challenges may arise, I am full of joy knowing that I am connected with God.

After Nehemiah managed oversight of the rebuilding of the wall, the exiles returned to Jerusalem. Ezra and other prophets stood from a platform and preached jointly from the Book of the Law to the people. They listened to the content and began to cry from the message given. It was then that Nehemiah stood before the people to remind them of the significance of the day:

> *"This day is holy to the* LORD *your God; do not mourn or weep." For all the people wept as they heard the words of the Law. Then he said to them, "Go your way. Eat the fat and drink sweet wine and send portions to anyone who has nothing ready, for this day is holy to our Lord. And do not be grieved, for the joy of the* LORD *is your strength.*
>
> —Nehemiah 8:9b-10

After all of the years of being away from their homeland, the Jewish people returned to a rebuilding and restoring scene. After witnessing the destruction of the wall and the defiling of the temple, the people were told to find joy in the Lord. Why? That joy would be their strength. Joy would be their courage to celebrate when completion had not yet materialized.

If I may push the idea, joy is the leaning post for hope and trust. Joy comes from our extensive knowledge of God and His ways. He has healed the sick, raised the dead, given sight to the blind, and prosperity to the poor. The Bible has documented it. People who serve God have confirmed it. We are the living embodiment of it. My knowledge of who God is and what He is able to do increases my excitement about Him. I am amazed that someone so vast and powerful takes the time to care about every element of my existence and intervenes when I am in need. That reality is a great reason to shout and praise God.

> I am amazed that someone so vast and powerful takes the time to care about every element of my existence and intervenes when I am in need.

Also, joy becomes a leaning post for hope and trust in the immediate moment. I know, believe, and experience the power of God. Trouble and trials attempt to shake my foundation. My hope and trust lean into my joy, because my joy is the seat of my knowledge and faith in God. Joy informs my hope and trust by saying, "If He did it before, He can do it again."

HIS ETERNAL REACH

Have you ever visualized God? I mean have you taken a moment to attempt to conceptualize the vastness of the Almighty? This psalm speaks of God as: Creator, Monarch, Shepherd, Merciful, Gracious, Ageless, and Enduring. These seven attributes don't scratch the scratches on the surface of our understanding of God.

Nevertheless, we are always to be reminded that God is much bigger than our ideas. We cannot box God. We cannot limit God. Consider the fact that the Lord sat on heaven's throne while conducting life-changing ministry among sinful flesh, through a spiritual power still not completely understood by Christians. That concept demonstrates extreme reach.

Many people debate about who is the greatest basketball player of all time. Sports reporters, fans, and barbershop experts everywhere have created many sets of criteria for anointing *the one*. The general consensus of greatness traits reflects skills, championship rings, stats, and leadership intangibles as signs of a great player.

Difficulty exists when we are pushed to dub number one. Michael Jordan was as clutch as they come. Kobe Bryant chucked many a jump shot, but five rings don't lie. Bill Russell set the standard for rings with the Celtics. LeBron James will be the king of Cleveland for delivering a title. Most of the greatness talk will be based on who your favorite player is.

My favorite basketball player is Earvin "Magic" Johnson. He was hanging on my door when I was a kid. I practiced my no-look passing skills because of him. I admired his game on the court. He was one of the few players in the NBA who could legitimately play all five positions on the court. He won championships and had epic rivalries.

Yet, Magic's basketball career was only a platform for his reach that is felt today. Johnson has demonstrated his business acumen through his many movie theaters, eating franchises, co-ownership of the Los Angeles Dodgers, and his most recent role as President of Basketball Operations for the Los Angeles Lakers. He is a husband, father, spokesman, businessman, entrepreneur, and a survivor of the challenges regarding his HIV diagnosis. His reach extends beyond one experience or environment.

Our praise increases and intensifies knowing that God is more than just our Savior. Our worship increases because we know that God is the same from age to age. He is willing to reveal greater levels of His glory. He is able to reach into our existence, because He cares about every element.

> *Are not two sparrows sold for a penny? And not one of them will fall to the ground apart from your Father. But even the hairs on your head are all numbered. Fear not, therefore; you are of more value than many sparrows.*
> —Matthew 10:29-31

Gratitude for His Grace and Mercy

Have you taken the time to tell the Lord, "Thank You"? What an unusual way to start off a thought. However, gratitude is something we do not always associate with praise or worship. It is easy to have an emotional response to what is happening around you. A chord or shout can prompt a dance. Gratitude is birthed out of a genuine feeling of *I don't deserve this*.

David was known as a man after God's own heart. David was the epitome of a worshipper. David is considered to be a primary psalmist of the Biblical Psalter with seventy-three songs credited to his penmanship. Yet, David had a moment where he missed the opportunity to worship God properly.

David had just retrieved the ark of the covenant from enemy occupation. So much elation came with regaining the presence of God. However, two problems existed. One, the ark was being carried on a cart rather than handled by the priest. Two, the lack of care for the ark caused the holy box to fall off the cart. In the process, a man attempted to save the relic from touching the ground, but he died trying to balance it his way. The thrill of victory and the agony of death took place because God was taken for granted.

David did not take the time to acknowledge his fault in the incident. Rather he decided to whine like a two-year-old and blame God for the tragedy. So David decided to pass the ark off to someone else. Now enters Obed-edom.

Obed-edom was not a major figure. He was a common man who was more than willing to embrace the presence of the Almighty. He was a common man who loved and worshipped an uncommon God. That thought should resonate with all of us. Obed-edom's decision to embrace the very presence of God yielded unusual favor for his household. One suggestion is made that the blessing on the home of Obed-edom was not only fiscally tangible but also reproductively prosperous. God went above and beyond for one who displayed genuine gratitude.

Of course, word reached David about the blessing God unleashed on Obed-edom. Imagine how stupid David felt hearing about these events. He recognized his error and returned back to Obed-edom's house. This time, David prepared properly and embraced God's presence with gratitude for another chance.

When we enter into the presence of God, we are not to mandate how the interaction should go. We are told to be thankful. We are told to praise God for His grace and mercy. We are in no position to dictate to God. The fact that you are reading these words is a sign of His mercy. The fact that I am writing these words is a sign of His grace. We could not engage this journey without God's consent.

For so many reasons, we must stop and examine our ways. We should not take for granted God's love. We should always be prepared to say thank you for all the things God has done. Hezekiah Walker wrote a song that embodies the nature of gratitude:

I am
Grateful for the things
That you have done
Yes, I'm grateful for the victories we've won
I could go on and on and on
About your works
Because I'm grateful, grateful, so grateful
Just to praise you Lord
Flowing from my heart
Are the issues of my heart
It's gratefulness [3]

No matter the season, struggle, or strife, never lose your ability to genuinely thank God for one more day. Remember to praise Him through everything. The blessing God has in store is ready to blow your mind. Relearn, then shout.

---

[3] Pastor Hezekiah Walker, "Grateful," *Lyrics.com*, https://www.lyrics.com/lyric/26848046/pastor+hezekiah+walker/grateful.

CHAPTER 4

DON'T MISINTERPRET MY STRUGGLE

> *And about the ninth hour Jesus cried out with a loud voice, saying, "Eli, Eli, lema sabachthani?" that is, "My God, my God, why have you forsaken me?" And some of the bystanders, hearing it, said, "This man is calling Elijah."*
>
> —Matthew 27:46-47

One of the worst things in the world that can happen to an individual is to be misunderstood. People have the tendency to react to individuals based on faulty information, learned or inherited bias, perception, or deep skepticism. Misunderstandings challenge our ability to see things or people for who they are because we are consumed with our often-misguided perspectives.

Please understand that I recognize that some people, circumstances, and issues are blatantly hostile. I never have to question a person's intentions when he or she calls me some racial slur or other derogatory term. Those emotions are clear. You don't have to worry about anyone creating a case for reasonable doubt when someone attacks your character or credibility without cause. Guilty is the proper verdict.

Allow me to pose this interrogative. How is it possible that we misinterpret or misunderstand the struggles that people face daily? We see people living and functioning under so many varied situations on a daily basis. Rich, poor, empowered, and maligned—these proxies of humanity all have a story that has brought them to their current station. Yet, we are not always granted access to the information that points to the complete picture of the journey in progress.

I have shared this story many times in my adult years. It is a reflection on processing the call to preach the Gospel. At fifteen, I wrestled with what it meant to commit my life to the preaching of the Gospel. Some extremely deep people will discuss the weight of the call, the adjustment in living, and other things. Trust me, all of that came into play. However, I was dealing with acceptance issues, self-esteem blocks in my mind and heart, and an inferiority complex. I had the typical teenage trials with a righteous call. How convenient.

The only thing I knew to do at that stage of my growth in God was go to the altar. I found myself at the altar on my knees asking God to help me. Heck, I had no clue what I was going to do as a preacher. Can anyone reading this honestly say that in the same position you would not feel the tension of social awkwardness on the horizon with this mission?

Going into ministry at an early age can be hazardous to your social growth and development. But, I was so compelled in my heart by God I kept seeking guidance. One Sunday at the altar, the presence of God arrested me. I just could not move. I had no other option. The prayers were prayed. The songs were sung. The benediction was offered. I remained.

As God and I were in deep confidence, the rushing of feet seeking audience with the pastor interrupted my peaceful experience. I must admit that I could not understand why people felt the importance of walking over me. I did not have a rational thought for anyone feeling the necessity to push anyone out of the way while that person is seeking God.

Over time, I realized a couple things. First, most people are not always in tune with the spiritual happenings taking place around them. Once *church* is over, a member's focus is squarely on being polite enough to get to dinner. Of all people, I do understand.

However, the second thought is what rubs me the wrong way. Most people assume that a visible demonstration of seeking God is too much. While I agree that we ought to be careful not to turn moments of pursuing God into opportunities to prove our piety to others, I also know that moments require more than just a *Thank You, Father God* or an *Oh, God of Abraham, Isaac, and Jacob* prayer.

After my experience at the altar, I didn't think I would need to go back the next week. Lo and behold, there I was weeping like an infant trying to understand this burden. Service ended, but something different took place. My pastor, Dr. Charles E. Booth, came down from the pulpit and stood in front of me. He placed himself between the people who might not know what I was facing in that moment and me.

Knowing the Mount Olivet Church, Pastor Booth has probably heard bits and pieces of this story. I don't believe I have ever told him the complete story.

However, I am forever grateful to the Lord for that moment over twenty years ago. In that moment, it was like God saying, "Let Me send somebody as a tangible presence of My love for you." I needed somebody to understand me. Pastor did.

Right now, many of you are seeking for relief from being misunderstood. You want somebody to get it. You want to be seen for whom you are deep within. You don't want others to dictate your story to the world only to seek a retraction later due to the use of alternative facts. Better put, you want others to *tell it right or don't tell it at all*.

May I offer you some good news? We are in great company when it comes to being misunderstood. Jesus is probably the most misinterpreted biblical figure of all time. Scholars take His words for granted. Believers take His statements as suggestion not commands. Jesus is not accepted for His divinity or His humanity in the magnitude that He should.

The scene at the cross provides a platform for Jesus being misinterpreted greatly. People who gathered to watch His demise listened to His cries and watched His body endure unearthly levels of agony. Jesus taking on the beatings, nails, spear, and spike would definitely bring on the normal response of human agony. Yet, this agony was the culmination of a deep, bloody prayer hours before.

As we come to this six-hour act of this Good Friday drama, many critics were attempting to find meaning to the many lines of this performance. Jesus declared before the audience about feeling that God had forsaken Him. But somehow, the pain and anguish of the moment was lost in the crowd's hearing because of bad translation.

Many people in the crowd suggested that Jesus was not crying in anguish to God. Not so. Apparently, Jesus was so delusional at the time that it was inferred that He was calling on Elijah to come through the ages and rescue Him from the cross. Examine with me the following miscues of the crowd:

1. Bad linguistic interpretation (They had no idea what Jesus was talking about)
2. Lack of recognition of a prophetic moment (In the midst of pain, Jesus was fulfilling a task)
3. Minimal knowledge of the immediate backstory in the Garden (God promised that the *woman's seed* [Genesis 3:15] would damage the head of the serpent)
4. Believing that Jesus would call for Elijah over Jehovah (No recognition of the relationship between Jesus and the Father)
5. Waiting for Elijah to show up (Looking for the wrong redeemer)

Every one of these attributes was a major failure. This wrong picture must serve as a reminder for all of us to be careful how we can attempt to understand struggles—internal, external, or corporate. The struggle before, during, and after the cross was not for or about Jesus. It was for the redemption of the world. Our struggles and challenges ultimately are not about or for us alone. The struggle is that someone may discover the power of God.

It's Not Your Struggle to Interpret

Humanity has not learned the art of keeping our opinions to ourselves. In the context of church life, personal information can be spread faster than a Crying Jordan meme. (An Internet meme could be anything from an image to an email or video file; however, the most common meme is an image of a person or animal with a funny or witty caption.)[4] Many people enter into assumed safe zones with the hope that God will help them through their anguish. Yet, many people continue their processing with compounded challenges.

To all of us who will assume the position of observer at some point, grant me this moment of sharing a piece of advice. Stay out of people's business! You and I are not deputized to assess someone in the midst of a challenge. Also, do not water down or minimize Scripture to justify your propensity to gossip and tear down. For God sake, do not force yourself on someone's life under the banner of *pious, super saint* status.

Throughout my years in the body of Christ, I have watched people examine the private struggles of many children of God. They diagnosed the situation without the anointing or discernment. They gave information without wisdom or prayer. They offered solutions without authorization from God. Ultimately, those reckless people aborted a portion of the journeys that God ordained for enhancement of those believers.

The crucifixion gatherers attempted to decipher the mind of God in their flesh while lacking a

---

[4] Vangie Beal, *webopedia*, "Internet meme," https://www.webopedia.com/TERM/I/internet_meme.html.

relationship with Him. Strange enough, relationship is the general key that will grant anyone access to the deep places where the soul resides. We cannot create relationships with people on the premise of being inquisitive. Relationship is birthed out of a genuine love and care fashioned by God.

> **Being engaged with God will teach us how to demonstrate the type of care that people need through painful moments.**

If we don't love God, we lack the capacity to love others. If we don't embrace what matters to God, we will not be able to decipher how to best appreciate and love others during seasons of distress. Being engaged with God will teach us how to demonstrate the type of care that people need through painful moments.

PURPOSE IN STRUGGLE

Every challenge or difficulty is not arbitrary. Things don't just happen when it comes to our spiritual development. Every single moment we experience as a child of God has relevance. It is not an easy existence. It is not a simple life. However, difficulty brings about a unique and colorful tapestry to our witness, deliverance, and liberation.

Before I began penning this section of work, I reflected on the sermon that represents the foundation of this particular chapter. The message was a part of a Seven Last Words service that took place years ago. For those who are not familiar, a Seven Last Words service takes place during Holy Week leading into the celebration of the resurrection of Jesus Christ.

This type of service is one of my personal favorites to witness and serve as a participant. One, it is a unique fellowship for preachers. Depending on the setup, a person can hear some of the sharpest, keenest theological minds address the thoughts of Christ on the cross, referred to as the final sayings of Jesus. Two, we have a chance to experience the catharsis of declaration and the healing in proclamation. Every preacher needs a word.

When my turn came to preach in this particular service, I was concerned with being clear in my thoughts and presentation. I had no idea how the Word would move. I had no inkling where this message would travel.

The end of the service came. Everyone was departing the church. At that moment, my friend, Pastor Ronald Chunn, stopped me. Pastor Chunn pulled me to the side and began to share with me how the message was a blessing to him. Needless to say, a young preacher was pleased that an experienced pulpiteer would share that sentiment. The next moment of the conversation, I will never forget.

A few months before our encounter, Ronald became a widower. His wife of over thirty years, Marion, transitioned from this side of life due to the difficult fight against cancer. Marion battled this disease on multiple occasions, but God granted her sweet relief from her suffering. She was a sweet, gentle woman. Every time I saw her at some district event, the grace and love of God was evident on her.

"Your message blessed me," Pastor Chunn said. "I have had so many people try to tell me how to feel about all of this. People have worried about me. They tried to tell me how to mourn and grieve. They have tried to tell my story."

I chimed in. "Nobody can tell you how to process your feelings."

Ronald took one look at me and said, "Exactly! I am better than what people think."

When you get to know someone, you learn certain things. You find out if people have humor, intelligence, and other intangible attributes. Somehow I knew that a gem of wisdom was about to come into my life. Pastor Chunn did not disappoint. "I am keeping to myself so I can process. Plus, I don't want to deal with the casserole ministry."

I was thoroughly confused. "Huh, the what?"

The good reverend exegeted this concept. "That's right. First, they drop off the casserole being nice. Then, they keep coming to get in your house. Young man, avoid it at all costs."

One conversation produced a richness of various emotions. I witnessed a man navigating through understandable pain, yet he never lost his smile or witness. Pastor Chunn said that God used me to bless him. I sincerely believe it was the reverse. Reading and studying in a seminary class will give you insight into exegetical practices, Biblical study methods, grief counseling, and other useful information about our faith walk. However, life puts our knowledge and information to the test daily.

We addressed earlier in this work the character Job. We always reference him when discussing difficulty, but let us reimagine the power of one statement he made, "Naked I came from my mother's womb, and naked shall I return. The LORD gave, and the LORD has taken away; blessed be the name of the LORD" (Job

1:21). Job considered his circumstances from a very unique position. He was prosperous, and lost his tangible prosperity. But, we discover that his inner foundation was secure in spite of physical loss.

> **One momentary difficulty should not define our present or our future. This period ought to be the unveiling of the power of God to sustain you.**

One momentary difficulty should not define our present or our future. This period ought to be the unveiling of the power of God to sustain you. The metal of our witness is never revealed during prosperity. Don't let people offer you incomplete theology. Prosperity (tangible and inner) is the reward for surviving the challenge. Troubles are the instruments to reveal your willingness to continue the journey.

THE GLORY AFTER THE STRUGGLE

Let us reset. Jesus is on the cross. He is suffering, bleeding, and dying a gruesome death. Prior to being nailed down, Jesus endured the beatings and carrying of the instrument of His earthly demise. Compounding the pain was the slow pace of the six hours of suspension from the cross. To add insult, Jesus was expressing emotional and physical agony, but people wanted to stay to witness if their terrible interpretation would materialize.

If being misunderstood is bad, someone waiting to see his or her interpretations of your situation come to pass in your life is downright awful. The people may have found it a little awkward to say to Jesus,

"Could You repeat that?" However, my level of cynicism informs my brain to consider that most of those particular people cared less about understanding. Many of the observers were not interested in what was truly taking place.

Take a step back and honestly look at the scene. Blood. Sweat. Tears. Thirst. Agony. Where is the salvation? Where is the redemption? Where is the healing for the nations? Where?

Though it is not explicit in the selected text, the whole story of the crucifixion brings about the *first conversion under the blood*. Two thieves engaged in a theological debate about the legitimacy of the Savior. One suggested that the miracle of self-removal from death would indicate validation to the claim of the Son of God. However, the other thief examined the argument as a mockery to the sovereignty, righteousness, and witness of Jesus.

The dissenting argument of this sinful man was followed by a unique request, "Jesus, remember me when You come into Your kingdom." The unnamed man did not ask for VIP status. He just wanted to be on the mind of the Lord at coronation time. Jesus looks back and says, "Today you will be with Me."

Amazing, don't you think? With all the pain and suffering taking place at that moment, Jesus had enough within to give this man what he needed—redemption. We say from pulpits everywhere that Jesus died that we might live. We say that the suffering Christ endured was that we might live. If only for the salvation of one, Jesus was willing to die for the one. It's a beautiful sentiment. Call me crazy, but I think the magnitude of the sacrifice can no longer be watered down.

In Genesis, the Creator began the elaborate process to redeem the most prized creation—humanity. Animal sacrifice could not appease. Legalism would not redeem. Human leaders demonstrated deep fallibility. Hope could not rest in any man-made entity. Politics do not work. Policy is riddled with agendas. Kingdoms do fall. The only thing that can save is the blood of Jesus.

> **The challenges of this moment are creating the tapestry of your breakthrough.**

In respect to my brothers and sisters who do not like the bloody nature of this type of atonement theory, allow me to say that I don't like it either. However, it is not because of the bloody gore of the imagery. I hate reading about the crucifixion story and being reminded that my sin caused this death. I hate reading that this execution caused my Savior to be an unrecognizable son to his mother. It is terrible that friends denied His presence, left Him in moments of vulnerability, and scattered out of fear. Jesus faced our sins alone.

Yet, the reason I embrace the pain is the payout in the end. Because Christ suffered, I have the opportunity to live forever. Because He rose, opportunity exists to live forever. Because He rose with scars, I know that my wounds will heal. Because Jesus rose, thank God Almighty, my life can experience the power of the resurrection every day.

Let us not take for granted the true glory on the other side of difficulties and misinterpretation. Your today may be horrible. Family is out of sorts. Job environment might be pressing every nerve ending in your body. Be of good cheer. The challenges of this moment are creating the tapestry of your breakthrough. This period of our lives is the one that will create the testimony that leads others to the cross. The struggle is real, but trouble doesn't last always.

CHAPTER 5

THE VALUE OF THE PROCESS: REAFFIRMED

> Jesus said, "Take away the stone." Martha, the sister of the dead man, said to him, "Lord, by this time there will be an odor, for he has been dead four days." Jesus said to her, "Did I not tell you that if you believed you would see the glory of God?" So they took away the stone. And Jesus lifted up his eyes and said, "Father, I thank you that you have heard me. I knew that you always hear me, but I said this on account of the people standing around, that they may believe that you sent me." When he had said these things, he cried out with a loud voice, "Lazarus, come out." The man who had died came out, his hands and feet bound with linen strips, and his face wrapped with a cloth. Jesus said to them, "Unbind him, and let him go."
>
> —John 11:39-44

I must confess that I thought this portion of the book could be confined to one chapter. Reflecting on the subject matter through various conversations, prayers, and meditation brought me to the conclusion that speaking on the anointing in any capacity cannot be a one-note enterprise. The Spirit of God has compelled me to address the oil of the anointing in two parts—reaffirmation and elevation.

Have you ever purchased a bookcase? Maybe the shelving was walnut or rich mahogany. Many bookshelves are usually packaged in a million pieces with instructions on how to put it together. The boxes labeled *E-Z assemble* are a tool of the devil. Somehow pieces are missing, and you are forced to find a way for the picture to materialize into reality.

Sounds like a moment of regret and frustration. You are correct. I have destroyed more $40 bookshelves than I can count. Okay, I am not the handiest person in the world. However, I am mentally competent enough to follow directions. Yet, I have discovered new ways to jack up a bookcase. No matter the amount of reading and following directions, I just can't seem to get the shelves right. After a moment of denial, I just determine that the product is defective. The truth is that user error is interfering with a finished bookshelf.

This very simple example demonstrates a general lack of patience for a process. Many times, we are more consumed by the fulfillment of a desired outcome than the steps toward it. The most logical and pragmatic individual understands the importance and value of proper steps.

Ponder this. A grilled cheese sandwich is only cheese and bread without a process. A car is nothing more than a collection of parts without an assembly process. A cake is floured salmonella surprise without heat. Gumbo is a bunch of meat, seafood, and stock without a roux. Process and procedure in any context is important and valuable.

One of the most important lessons I have learned in ministry is making certain the anointing of God is a part of my continued growth and development. The subject of the anointing has been a perplexing one for many years in the life of the church. People have found themselves on a continuum when it comes to personal attachment and understanding.

As a disclaimer, I do not count myself as a deeper authority on the subject than other contemporaries. This moment is an opportunity to share a concept that I have studied, experienced, and continues to grow by revelation. At best, my goal is to enhance a believer's awareness regarding being anointed and the anointing.

The anointing has been reduced, in many faith circles, to being an element of being set apart by God. Preachers, prophets, bishops, and other leaders hang their hats on being anointed by God. That realm of understanding is reasonable and rational. People are set apart for service to God.

Yet, I wonder when we are going to place an emphasis on the need for fresh oil. Yes, the oil gives us a *slick and shiny* identifying mark of being chosen by God. Eventually, the oil dries up and the evidence is not as clear. If that is true, is it possible that we have taken our anointed status for granted? Has our positioning numbed our ability to see that we need something new from God?

Come on in here, Fried Chicken. Talk to us about good oil.

"Well, Brother Preacher, fresh oil enhances my coating, color, flavor, and cooking temperature. Overused oil can become rancid and diminish my process. Bad oil affects my outcome. If my normal cooking time is twelve minutes, good oil will produce the desired experience for the consumer. If you leave me in some bad oil, my appearance may cause you to pull me out too soon. I will be undercooked and cause terrible digestive issues for anyone who consumes me. Leave me in too long, I will be finished on the inside but burnt on the outside. Fresh oil is important."

> **Every new challenge compels us to yield to a fresh prospective of the Holy Spirit's leading.**

Much like the fried chicken motif suggests, the most pious, righteous believer needs an oil change. Just like a car engine, you and I can only go so far with our current oil situation. No, I am not saying that God's oil is limited. I am suggesting that we must be careful assuming that the oil we have suits every encounter.

Let me step back. God processes our purpose, destiny, and position in the Kingdom of God. The Creator puts us through the paces to prepare us for greater responsibilities and challenges. We are not sent without help. The Holy One anoints us to show the measure of who we are through God.

The initial process helped us arrive at this unique point in our lives. Why would we ever believe that we could only rest on one moment? Why would anyone live believing he or she was no longer in need of a refreshing? Stages of growth mandate a fresh coat of oil. Every new challenge compels us to yield to a fresh prospective of the Holy Spirit's leading. Every moment with God is not strictly about ceremony. It is necessary that we find comfort and peace in the affirmation of God.

Chapters 11 and 12 of John are the bookends of an unfolding adjustment in a friendship. We always navigate toward the scene where Jesus is having His feet anointed by Mary. The act of Mary was a significant moment in the journey that Christ would make toward the cross. However, we do not always take into account the magnitude of the act.

In order to understand the table scene better, we must reexamine the desperate call of Mary and Martha in chapter 11. The two sisters sent word to Jesus about the condition of their brother, Lazarus. Jesus' friend was in a dire state. They didn't want anyone else to address their brother's condition but Jesus. The rub became that Jesus did not move quickly. He took His time.

The disciples begged their teacher to move faster. Jesus decided to give information about the condition of Lazarus. He told them that things needed to get worse before God would demonstrate His power. Once word came that Lazarus died, Jesus moved. He made His way to a familiar place to perform a peculiar task.

Nobody took the time to inform these sisters of the plans of God. They were mourning and preparing to bury their brother. They built resentment and hostility toward the man they called *friend*. Look at the dynamics between Mary and Jesus. Mary was the one person that made it a point to sit at the feet of Jesus. She neglected other tasks just to be around for the teaching. She could never get enough of this fresh revelation. Now, the fire had been put out.

Jesus arrives with the knowledge and insight that Lazarus would be resurrected. He came fully prepared to bring His friend back from burial preparation and decay. Upon arrival, His presence was not welcomed. Mary said that His power was needed days ago to prevent this tragedy. Mary vocalized that they didn't want secondhand movement.

The grief that Mary felt in that moment turned into resentment. The ceremonial oil given at the baptism by John the Baptist became a rancid stench in the nostrils of Mary. Her anger was not generated by a lack of faith or trust. On the contrary, the knowledge of Jesus' power pushed them to send word to Him in the first place.

We need to journey and take seriously the idea He was as we were.

Let us not gloss over what was just said. I realize that the very suggestion that the Anointed One lacking oil may border on lunacy and possible heresy. However, I implore you to take a moment to look at this scene through a different scope for just a second. (Forgive me in advance for what might appear to be a defense in a seminary course.)

We must begin with a general premise that is accepted in most Christian circles. Jesus was the 100/100 man—100 percent human and 100 percent divine. We generally deal more with the divinity of Jesus than the humanity of the Son of God. Yes, it is a challenge given all that the Bible documents. Nevertheless, we need to journey and take seriously the idea *He was as we were.*

We must embrace the gift that is before us. Outside of salvation, the humanity of Jesus is the single, greatest gift Christ gives us. Think about it. We still live in this world, and we must navigate through the pitfalls and insanity of it. The fact that Jesus lived through all of this turmoil lets me know that God has given us everything necessary to make it.

For the purpose of a different perspective, Jesus was sitting in a position where He was previously affirmed before people. Now, people who loved Him questioned His status. Jesus stood in need of being reaffirmed as a viable vessel for the people.

At some point in life, every person is in need of God reminding him or her that they are valuable to the Kingdom of God and the environment where they are planted. We cannot skip the aspect of reaffirmation, because we will not fully embrace or appreciate what God has in store for us.

> **Outside of salvation, the humanity of Jesus is the single, greatest gift Christ gives us.**

Jesus is approaching the grave of Lazarus. The grief of a friend's death, joined with the disappointment of a sister/friend, and the spectators who were only present for the repast, provided the breeding ground for tears. Jesus was dealing with real emotions that may have challenged His inner resolve. I am willing to push the idea that the man was dealing with a moment of soul struggle. The emotional baggage might bring about greater meaning to the prayer that Jesus prayed at that moment:

> *Father, I thank you that you have heard me. I knew that you always hear me, but I said this on account of the people standing around, that they believe you sent me.*
> —John 11:41b-42

Jesus addresses why He was at the grave. By taking this step, the Savior brings to our attention the tension between being anointed and the environment questioning that truth. The friction of those ideas presents the following concepts:

1. Jesus actively sought reaffirmation from the Father.
2. Jesus acknowledged the people required more than intellectualized faith.
3. His relationship with the Father gave Him the strength to hold on to what He knew.

Now, we know the end of this part of the story. A decomposing Lazarus was regenerated into a living, viable person. But, that result is not the *what* we must examine. Let us break down how the steps of reaffirmation can lead us toward the moments of victory and miracles.

Addressing Rancid Emotions

As it was stated earlier, Mary was sick of Jesus. The death of her brother exposed the reality that faithful believers can suddenly dwell in their feelings. Mary's devotion to Jesus appeared to have died along with Lazarus. We can say that her disillusion prematurely buried her faith. That opinion is based on us sitting as outside observers. However, it was very possible that Mary totally wrote off Jesus due to a less than favorable response.

Here comes a rough moment of truth. We do not always gain a favorable response to our difficulty. I question anyone who can say without fail that God has given them an affirmative answer to every prayer. If that were true, I would be rich, with a car for every day, and four homes representing each geographical direction.

Jesus was anointed. Jesus had the power to do anything. Jesus was the fleshly manifestation of the Godhead. But, He was questioned by the faithful. If that challenge confronted Jesus, we should breathe easier. Why? Human expectations are based upon what one knows. Knowledge is limited. That limitation potentially creates very toxic encounters. Toxic encounters produce rejection.

Mary reacted based on her interactions, knowledge, and conviction. She governed herself according to the oil presented. She trusted the validity of the anointing. She embraced the power of the anointing. Yet, an apparent change in the approach of Jesus caused Mary to see everything Jesus presented as a reproach to her sensibilities.

Imagine being in Mary's shoes. Questioning everything you ever heard from someone you trusted to feed your spirit. Consider the heartbreak you might feel seeing your request being denied or your acute emotions being placed in mental deferment. Wait. Many of us know this feeling. We place these emotional responses and expectations on pastors, leaders, teachers, elders, and others.

Let's be honest. We have thought and expressed ourselves in this manner on many occasions. We have reacted out of our perspective and not God's reality. We must unpack the emotional from the truth.

The guiding principle of spiritual leadership is that the Holy Spirit leads leaders. Leaders who are led by God are subject to taking turns that others will not initially understand. Take this simple example. A pastor is preaching and teaching the paint of the wall of a local church. The congregation loves the move of God through the pastor. They are benefiting in many dimensions—spiritual, numerical, emotional, and fiscal.

Suddenly, the decision is made to eliminate the printing of bulletins for worship. *Why would you do that?* The pastor explains how people never read them, and they are nothing but a distraction. A more efficient method has been developed so the worship experience can flow and receive the reverence it deserves. Now, the people who loved the Word so much change their mind about the vessel, because no more paper would exist in worship.

> **Moving according to the will of God can cause a situation to become toxic before experiencing a fresh perspective.**

Some people would say (and I have heard this throughout my ministry), "You can't force change on people." While that might be true most of the time, I submit to you exhibit A—Jesus. "But, Reverend, that's not fair. He's Jesus." Once again, Jesus is our example. Jesus decided, without consulting His friends, to follow the plan of His Father recognizing the roadblocks ahead.

Moving according to the will of God can cause a situation to become toxic before experiencing a fresh perspective. To use the fried chicken motif, imagine looking at a deep fryer full of used oil. In that oil, you will see particles of previously fried chicken. The amount of usage makes the oil black and full of the past. If the oil is not changed, the chicken will be fried in the remnants of the past, altering the taste.

Mary was leaning so heavily on previous encounters that she was potentially poisoning her opportunity to appreciate Jesus in a new manner. Interesting. She wanted the same *flavor*, but could not get it. She rejected Jesus because the oil was finished, but she was not prepared to go through the process for a fresh experience.

We must be careful not to lead with our emotions concerning God. We might be in a position to witness the power of an oil change. We must be mindful that if the *taste* is off, God is letting us know that better is coming if we wait. Jesus would be reaffirmed because the past experience was no longer enough.

REFILLED PURPOSE

So we recognize that the relationship with Christ was becoming routine. Jesus was anointed, but freshness was in order. Jesus cried out to the Father with a purpose. He knew before arriving that this defining moment would arrive. Jesus stated that what was about to take place was that the people might believe that He was sent.

In the acute moment, Jesus was present to raise Lazarus from the dead. The people needed evidence of Jesus' validity as the Son of God. Affirmation was necessary. It arrived through a demonstration of power. But, we must focus on the prayer that stated His need to be filled again.

Look at the stage that was set. Jesus asked for the stone to be moved. The smell of decomposition was filling the air. Doubt rose among the spectators. Curiosity crept into the proceedings. We all know people were waiting for Jesus to fall on His face.

The interesting thing about Jesus is that nobody could ever catch Him slipping. The setup was so great, but the Word would never let Jesus fail. In order to perform this miracle, Jesus needed it to be sanctioned by the Father. The precedent was established, but the complete understanding would be received later.

> *For I have not spoken on my own authority, but the Father who sent me has himself given me a commandment—what to say and what to speak.*
> —John 12:49

What a lesson for all of us. Unsanctioned movement by those who are anointed can be a hazardous scene. Prior to the moment, Jesus was confident in the following elements leading to this miracle:

1. Lazarus had to die.
2. Glory would come out of the situation.
3. The Father wanted the scene set in this manner.
4. The miracle does not occur without prior approval.

I remember my freshman year of high school. I was on the basketball team as a starting power forward. My main objective was to control the paint. My skills began to develop to the degree that I became a viable scoring option. My coaches saw my development and made sure I was active in the offense.

On opening night, my team was in a dogfight with an undermanned opponent. We should have blown them out, but we took them for granted. The game was tied with a few seconds left in the game. During our final time-out, I did something unusual. I asked for the ball in the final seconds. On this night, I welcomed the pressure.

However, my desire to win could only be affirmed by my coaches. I had the confidence that I could score, but they had to say yes. If my coaches said no, I would not have the ball. If they said no and I went for the win anyway, my arrogance might have cost us a victory.

My coaches affirmed my desire and demonstrated confidence in my talent. That night, I hit the only game-winning shot I ever attempted. After twenty years, I still remember that reverse layup and stat line; but those two points at the end of the game were the most meaningful. It was not about the time when the scoring took place. It was the coaches saying, "We believe."

> **Nothing can match the Creator of all saying, "Your purpose is valuable. I'm going to endorse it."**

Nothing in this world can match anyone telling you, "Go for it." Nothing can match the Creator of all saying, "Your purpose is valuable. I'm going to endorse it." When we feel like we will not make it, God sets moments like these to revive us. Why must it be full of high stress? I have no idea. Yet, God decides to use this level of perceived foolishness to get a glorious point across about His glory.

New Oil, New Assignment

So, a relationship was strained, because it was not functioning in an accepted fashion. Jesus was putting everything on the line in order to grant fresh revelation to all who would receive. This appointed time was to solidify the claim that Jesus was present for a reason. Jesus was going to call a dead man back from the grave.

I know what you are saying. Jesus was already raising the dead. Yes, the widow's son was awakened on the way to the burial ground (Luke 7). Jesus was accustomed to performing miracles when the time called for it. Yet, something was different about this moment.

Lazarus was good and dead. His body was returning back to earth. His body was presenting a stench in the atmosphere. We are not talking about a sanitary situation. It was the ugliest, nastiest, and possibly illegal (according to the Jewish law) circumstances possible. Perfect.

When Jesus opened His mouth and said, "Lazarus, come out," I imagine there was a holy hush over the crowd. What would they see? What would they not see? Three words would determine the relevance of Jesus. Three words would dictate the advancement of His ministry.

After the command went forth, a bound man came out, no longer smelling like death. Men unwrapped an individual who lost the look of departure. Lazarus was restored by a word with fresh oil. The people knew that Jesus was more than a man of God. They witnessed a new movement active in Him.

This entire journey of God's reaffirmation of Jesus had a high cost attached. The process in our lives will not always be pretty. Unfortunately, people will be removed for a season and maybe permanently. This time of growth and stretching will crush our preconceived notions about God.

Nevertheless, the pain and difficulty is used to press out new oil for a new moment in our lives. Preaching is different with fresh oil. Your witness is profound with fresh oil. Greater works take place with fresh oil. Relationships grow stronger with fresh oil. New oil brings about a jump-start to the next assignment. Newly pressed oil is the ultimate affirmation of our purpose and destiny in God. The oil leads us forward to the next stage—elevation.

Chapter 6

The Value of the Process: Elevated

> *Mary therefore took a pound of expensive ointment made from pure nard, and anointed the feet of Jesus and wiped his feet with her hair. The house was filled with the fragrance of the perfume. But Judas Iscariot, one of his disciples (he who was about to betray him), said, "Why was this ointment not sold for three hundred denarii and given to the poor?" He said this, not because he cared about the poor, but because he was a thief, and having charge of the moneybag he used to help himself to what was put into it. Jesus said, "Leave her alone, so that she may keep it for the day of my burial. For the poor you always have with you, but you do not always have me."*
>
> —John 12:3-8

May I share something in confidence? The majority of my existence has been governed by the pursuit of achievement. Ingrained in my psyche is the mantra of Ricky Bobby in *Talladega Nights*: "If you're not first, you're last!" (I like mindless movies.) At one point in my life, my competitive juices would silence my compassion. I could not stand a person that did not *have heart*.

Part of my problem was learning that settling was never an option. To this day, it is difficult for me to watch sports without a critical eye. Being competitive meant achieving the objective by any cost. My zest and desire to be number one has been tempered by a sobering reality. Being the best does not mean you are in the place of your purpose. Simply put, being the best at everything is not always a fit for a purpose.

I could run down the list of various skills and talents I possess. Many people might be shocked by the many things I can do. Yet, my purpose in this life has never been to be the most talented or gifted person in the room. My purpose is to aid in elevating people toward their destinations in life.

Brothers and sisters, I will not blatantly lie and tell you this revelation came to me in some high-definition dream sequence similar to Solomon. My arrival at this juncture was not birthed out of some great revival meeting, seminary class, or other profound setting. This moment of clarity has been generated through many experiences.

When I was attending Kentucky State, I made many friends and connections as most college students do. While you are going through the grind, you may not always see the potential or future of the individuals you meet. But, I met a brother named Terrance Green.

Terrance is a Midwest boy like me. He is originally from Detroit. My man is one of the smartest and most energetic men I have ever met in any age bracket. We were in many of the same circles. He loves God. Loves his hometown. He is my kind of guy.

One day, I was walking on *the* yard (campus) on my way to the library. Terrance saw me in the distance. I heard someone yell toward me, "Bishop!" (People have called me Bishop since high school.) We greeted each other like brothers do. We carried on a conversation. You know the normal stuff. Honestly, I don't remember every detail. All I recall was that we encouraged each other and went on about our business.

Time moves on about ten years from that moment. Social media provided the opportunity to reconnect with my friend. We chatted through instant messages. We caught up and talked about graduate and doctoral work. I shared how proud I was of the strides he was making through his PhD work. Like I said, he is a beast in life and intellect.

In the course of the conversation, the strangest occurrence took place. *I will never forget that conversation in front of Blazer* (library), Terrance typed. *Thank you for your encouragement.* I still have no recall to the entire exchange that took place in front of the library. Apparently, the timing of the encounter helped my brother not to give up. Maybe it was just a reminder to keep pursuing the purpose on his life. But, years later this moment in time still resonated with him.

This whole string of moments reminds me that every child of God needs affirmation and preparation for elevation. It would be extremely pretentious on my part to believe or suggest that one conversation with me elevated a man who is now an associate professor at a major university in Texas. I am very confident that this intellectual powerhouse had a support system that remains more vast.

Yet, I take the position that everyone who walks with God will have a Mary come along to accent the reality of what God has placed in you. Someone will figuratively wipe your feet with his or her hair. It will be someone fully acquainted with your journey that will definitively declare the greatness and purpose that lives within you.

> **I take the position that everyone who walks with God will have a Mary come along to accent the reality of what God has placed in you.**

Let us unfold the aftermath of Lazarus' resurrection. After Jesus spoke life back into the decomposing frame that housed the essence of Lazarus, a collection of disjointed responses was produced. Many people were amazed at the miracle that took place. Hope was restored. Faith increased for many people. A friendship was strengthened. But, anger and resentment took hold of the religious hierarchy.

We acknowledge that Jesus was ultimately sent to earth to die in our place. Sin had to be conquered. Life had to be offered to the lost. However, this event increased the efforts of the jealous and insecure to eliminate Jesus and Lazarus from the view of the hopeless and maligned.

> *Sidenote moment: Whenever God performs an unusual work in our lives, we can expect discounters, haters, or whatever label we can use, to attempt to discredit the momentum of the move of God.*

The plans that were being formed were nothing but an opportunity for God to use evil's attempt at creativity. Nothing was done at the moment, but Jesus had a sense of His demise being on the horizon. Which brings us to the dinner table.

After the tirade that Mary displayed, she needed to present a different attitude. You know how it is. You blow smoke as to how you feel something should go. Then, you see everything take place totally opposite of your opinion, and everything works out. Yeah, we have all digested many feathers from that grade A crow. Mary was finished with her avian-brand meal. She decided to do something significant as a sign of commitment and love for Jesus.

Mary found something so expensive that it cost a year's salary. She broke out some oil and anointed the feet of Jesus. She took the extra step of performing this act with her hair rather than a towel or cloth. Mary was not summoned by Jesus to carry out this deed. Mary was not being used as a pawn for patriarchal domination. Independent conviction led her to paint the feet of Jesus.

This one act has been discussed in church life for hundreds of years. People have discussed every aspect of the scene. We see an unsanitary act. We acknowledge the greed of Judas as he watches a commodity being wasted. We discuss the cost of the oil. Yet, I do not believe we talk enough about the correlation between the act and the proclamation of Jesus' pending meeting with the cross.

In many ways, we do not always catch the hint from God about the activities happening around us. Someone who compliments you might be doing something more than just being nice. The acknowledgment of your talent may be more than an observation. Moments happen at times to be indicators of pending elevation. Those moments might be the runway toward the next stage of your purpose.

This moment in our lives is an opportunity to witness not when but how God will elevate our condition. When we meet our launching place of elevation, God will intentionally set off a signal by the scent of His oil that change is taking place. Our current condition will change by God lifting us to a new place.

Identify Under the Anointing

My life has been covered with many names. My *government* name is Charles Walter Ferguson. Childhood yielded C. W. as my moniker. Charles was accepted in school life. Dr. Ferguson has been used in the classroom. I'm Charlie or Pooh to my wife. (If you try to say either in public without her written consent, she will harm you!) C. J. calls me, Daddy. However, the name that I am beginning to embrace is the pen name on the front of this book, Dr. C. Walter Ferguson.

When I was ten years old, I made my confession of faith at the Mount Olivet Baptist Church. Dr. Booth is one of the smartest and most articulate individuals that has ever graced this planet. I love my pastor. His scholarship is impeccable. The repository of knowledge stored in his mind is unmatched. But, even the greatest minds have a bad day.

June 7, 1992 was the date of my baptism. It was an unbelievable day. Family was at the house for a huge dinner. Everyone was excited. I mean it was the first adult decision I ever made. Serving God is not a small throwaway concept. I believed with my whole heart that hell was no longer an option. Heaven would be my home.

My family and I arrived at the church to prepare for my baptism. Nerves did not bother me. Water was cold for a second, but that feeling passed quickly. I stood in the pool with one of my heroes. I was fine. "In obedience to that great commission," Pastor Booth began, "and on the confession of your faith, I baptize you, my brother in Christ, Charles Wilson Ferguson, in the name of the Father, and of the Son, and of the Holy Ghost." Who is that? Did my name just morph?

I know it was a simple mistake that makes for a funny highlight in my life. It is also the prompt that sparked the creation of my pen name. For all I know, Dr. Booth may not have remembered the moment until reading these pages. Yet, it provides an interesting view on identity.

Jesus sitting at a table with other people was a common occurrence. Teaching people in homes or other intimate settings was Jesus' forte. Being seen in a greater light was not abnormal for Him. However, Jesus' purpose being put in the forefront in an atmosphere like this one was not a normal act.

The anointing brought His saving and redeeming cause before the people in a more significant manner. The followers would have to address the reality that this current state of Jesus' ministry would no longer be the norm. This act identified Jesus as a replacement to atone for our mess as humanity.

Hear the words of Jesus again. *Leave her alone. She bought it so that she might keep it for the day of my burial.* The pseudo-concern for the poor was trounced by the future of death to come on the horizon. Jesus said that the work of the Kingdom will remain, but I must finish my objective first.

The anointing accounts for everything we are today and identifies who we shall be tomorrow. The lesson that we must continue to learn every day is not to be afraid when God calls us for assignment. It means the Creator believes we are ready for the next steps. Like a hard-working minor league baseball prospect, we are waiting for the call. However, doing the work until the call comes will guarantee the opportunity.

THE COST AND REALITY OF ELEVATION

The teenage years were an interesting time of my life. I had a normal adolescent experience except for the preaching ministry hiccup at sixteen. I mean seriously. What kid in his or her right mind chooses this life that early? I still contend some days that somebody close to me drugged me somehow. I am kidding... somewhat. However, my life has accrued serious cost for serving the Lord.

As a teen, my dating life was really specific. The girl had to be a church girl. I could not deal with anyone who appeared to be less than holy. Well, at least that was the mentality I needed to carry since most girls were not attracted to the exegesis of the biblical text. The collar might have been a deterrent. I was aware that my life would be different forever. I just did not have a clue how true that would be. Everything changed.

The words of Pastor Booth come back to my memory. He introduced me on the night of my initial sermon. In classic Booth fashion, the intro was, if not, more profound than the sermon. "I want to share with you tonight that ministry is not a boy's job. I know he is young, but he is assuming a man's task."

At that very moment, my anxiety reached a million. That statement was not rendered to incite fear. Rather the message was to convey the seriousness of the call I was undertaking.

For nearly two decades, I can say without any hesitation, those words have been the most revealing and prophetic collection I have ever embraced. Ministry is not easy. Serving God is not simple. I don't care when you embraced your God-given purpose. I could care less about how long you ran from it. Ministry is not a self-serving enterprise.

Yes, people have come along and bastardized the power and influence provided to do great work. Of course, some individuals saw this life as a second career and not a calling (which by the way is a derogatory, preposterous, and outlandish take on the spreading of the Gospel). Some people water down the magnitude of serving God in this manner. It does not change the reality. Ministry is a challenge.

Okay. You're not a preacher reading this book. Yes, ministry is not limited to the proclamation of the Gospel. Ministry is service. If you serve with your whole heart, you have felt the heaviness and difficulty that comes with serving the Lord.

Maybe you are just doing your best to live a life worthy of the saving grace of God. You know the cost. Many people who were close to you fell off the face of the earth. Your inner circle became smaller. The *seventy-two* you associate with (ref. Luke 10) are not faces of great influence. Recognize living for the Lord brings about unusual challenges.

Beloved, don't lose heart. The disruption is your normal, the fragrance of newness; and the signals of change are the signs to shift your attention. It is time to possess peak awareness about what is taking place.

Examine the scene at Bethany one more time. Mary anoints. Judas complains. Jesus corrects. Jesus calls Mary's act one that will be remembered forever. Jesus refers to Judas' explanation of the needs of the poor as a constant work. Jesus did not erase the significance of tending to the disenfranchised. In an interesting manner, Jesus reminded a greedy man of his responsibility.

Jesus knew the price of the oil. It had a financial, emotional, relational, and spiritual cost attached. He knew the price attached to being elevated. Jesus would have to die in humiliating fashion. His family would not recognize Him. But, the reward of the elevation was great.

> *Now is the judgment of this world; now will the ruler of this world be cast out. And I, when I am lifted up from the earth, will draw all people to myself.*
> —John 12:31-32

Elevation has a price, but it is only an initial investment. Focusing on what we may lose can deter us from the genuine payoff. Yes, Jesus had a moment of reassessing. Yes, He asked the Father for other options. However, Jesus was prepared for that elevation in advance.

Inevitably, we will question why this manner and method exist. Nights will be sleepless at times. Tears will be shed. Objects will absorb our anger. Just don't forget about your anointing moment.

Reflect on how God blessed you by saying, "I choose you." Remember the peace of knowing the

Lord will never leave you nor forsake you in the journey. God has promised us to be with us in every step of the journey. God is ready to grant us the oil, but only the willing can truly receive it.

Chapter 7

Overcoming Uncertainty

> *Now the birth of Jesus Christ took place in this way. When his mother Mary had been betrothed to Joseph, before they came together she was found to be with child from the Holy Spirit. And her husband Joseph, being a just man and unwilling to put her to shame, resolved to divorce her quietly. But as he considered these things, behold, an angel of the Lord appeared to him in a dream, saying, "Joseph, son of David, do not fear to take Mary as your wife, for that which is conceived in her is from the Holy Spirit. She will bear a son, and you shall call his name Jesus, for he will save his people from their sins."*
>
> —Matthew 1:18-21

Many competencies are rooted in the realm of the unknown. Many people who participate in public speaking deal with many challenges before approaching a crowd. An individual works diligently on subject matter that should appeal to the crowd. While processing the element of the speech of presentation, the speaker edits, considers time constraints, and other potential difficulties. The process can be strenuous and daunting.

Yet, the moment arrives when the presenter finally reaches a place of peace about everything. The mind echoes the chant, *You can do it!* The heart is in the rhythm of agreement. The whole body is moving in unison, until the eyes catch the view of the crowd. *Retreat!* scream our eyes. The fear embedded in that cry ushers in uncertainty.

Amazing. A person works hard to get the nerve and confidence to stand before a group of listeners only to feel stationary when the time arrives. Why would that occur? He or she knows that the group found him or her. It is believed that this individual is competent to discuss whatever is needed. Why would that speaker suddenly second-guess his or her ability to execute the objective?

At least one answer for our consideration is that every person deals with doubt. It is okay, super-spiritual people. Everyone is confronted by doubt. Come out and be delivered. It is fine to actually declare the following phrase: "I have doubt."

Doubt has a useful place in our existence when applied properly. I doubt that I will go for a tryout with an NFL team. I believe I have the acumen for football. I believe I have a work ethic to get in the proper shape for a multimillion-dollar contract. However, doubt is connected to a reality. I am moving toward the age of forty. My body does not bounce back like it did at eighteen.

Many people doubt the ability of the government to protect the interests of the people. Why? As long as individual interests are more profitable than the advancement of all, the government will never meet minimal expectations. A government for the people is only a concept if the people have nothing or no one seeking the common good.

I might concede that the examples of doubt might be a better form of healthy skepticism. In any view, doubt can reveal our deepest fears, broken dreams, insecurities, and a myriad of elements addressing the deep, inner places of our hearts. Doubt has a use.

The problem we face is how to deal with doubt or uncertainty in a healthy way. Think about the times doubt entered your life to destroy your purpose, hope, or dreams. Let us say, young, single man or woman, you are back on the dating scene. Your friends finally convinced you that TGIT, DVR'd shows, video games, and junk food are not the tools to attract a potential mate.

> **Doubt can reveal our deepest fears, broken dreams, insecurities, and a myriad of elements addressing the deep, inner places of our hearts.**

You finally put on your *go to meeting* clothes and leave your home. Your friends take you to a nice restaurant where they set you up with someone you don't know. Yes, it is the dreaded blind date. However, this blind date is not the ordinary pairing. Check this out.

Sisters, your girls found the man you always talked about. He is in the class of Idris Elba, Channing Tatum, David Beckham, Denzel Washington, and whoever clears your fineness test. The man has a job with a 401k. He has no relationship drama, loves his mama, helps the community, and loves the Lord.

Brothers, this woman could walk around with Serena Williams, Paula Patton, Scarlett Johansson,

Janelle Monae, or Taraji P. Henson. She makes her own money. She is only digging for gold out of her own purse. Her personality would give you a cavity. She walks with grace and humility. Loves God and people. She can kick it with the fellas and talk it up with the Fortune 500.

These people fit the dreams and visions you have. But, a problem exists. The memory of your tired, ignorant ex invades your cognitive space. Your eyes see the baddest person you have ever seen; but this recall to the past becomes a cataract to the future you want. The grief, anger, and disappointment overtake your heart. Doubt sets up residence and tells you, *This is too good to be true. It will end like the last time.*

We begin to believe that anything about our lives might be a waste of time. According to Doubt, Promise and Possibility are nothing but jokes. Doubt says that we are beyond the stages of being helped. We are past our opportunity for joy or happiness. Doubt reinforces our deepest worries by asking Fear to agitate our pain.

Moments like these are common in our valley condition. Being away from the normal ebb and flow of life will give us room to dwell on what has not happened, what we don't deserve, and what we have not accomplished. We wallow in our feelings believing that nothing will come out of the time or season in between blessings. Yet, we are hoping for a way out of these difficult inner confrontations. What provisions exist to overcome doubt?

Existing in Scripture is the saga of the arrival of Jesus into the world. If not for my faith in Christ, I would consider this plan to bring the Savior into the world convoluted, unreasonable, and unnecessary. I guess that is why I am the created, not the Creator. However, I do not believe that it is harmful to critique and examine the circumstances surrounding the birth of Christ.

Matthew's account of the arrival of Christ highlights a person that does not receive enough attention in my opinion—Joseph. We understand the importance of Mary. Our Catholic brothers and sisters place significant emphasis on Mary as being holy. Naturally, Mary was important because she was the chosen vessel to carry the Christ child. But, what about Joseph?

This man was in love with a young woman that was pregnant. The love of Joseph's life was carrying a child that would have no DNA attachment to Joseph. Can you imagine what the conversation might have been between Mary and Joseph? Can you imagine Mary trying to convince a man that she loves that this pregnancy shouldn't come between them? What a dilemma.

The Scripture presents us with a challenging moment of emotional, mental, and spiritual stress. Matthew suggests that Joseph took account of the entire situation. He saw the lay of the land, and it was not good. The whole set of issues was not granting much peace for Joseph's mind.

Joseph loved Mary. He looked at her and said that she was the one. Nobody else would do. His full emotional investment was in Mary. Yet, the law (religious and social) suggested that love was not enough. The law said that Joseph's manhood had been embarrassed and demeaned. Joseph would be seen as less of a man if he stayed. The law said to reestablish his status. Joseph would only regain his manhood and face by publicly humiliating Mary. Nothing was looking good.

Every aspect of this story has always made this moment in Scripture intriguing to my theological mind. Consider some of the questions and themes that are found in the text:

1. How destructive can a belief system be if your social acceptance is based on the suffering and humiliation of another person?
2. Godly love does not outweigh the law.
3. Doubt can place you between a rock and a hard place.
4. Only God can fix a mess like this.

Joseph was being forced to make a decision. His foundational knowledge and familiar environment influenced his understanding of love and faith. He made up his mind that he would divorce Mary in a private manner so she would not experience the overt humiliation granted by the public. I cannot imagine Joseph was content with his conclusion, but I guess it was the one that made the most sense according to his prior knowledge and understanding.

A funny thing happens when we take God out of the operation. The Creator finds a way to interject the necessary opinion. God stops Joseph's attempted follow-through by giving Joseph inside information. God lays out the plan that required Joseph to stand in as proxy for God to handle all of the necessary cultural requirements of fatherhood. More importantly, God trusted Joseph to protect the interest of redemption by marrying the love of his life and being father to Jesus.

The proposition was not an easy one. Joseph would be enduring major blows to his persona. Joseph would not be seen as a typical man according to unreasonable cultural norms of the day. No, Joseph would be walking out a mandate that signified him as God's man. To carry out the mandate, Joseph was given three things—a word, clarity, and a promise.

The Word Still Works

The largest part of this encounter between God and Joseph was the spoken Word of God. Joseph did not have the complete view of God's plan. Joseph was going to function out of limited understanding. Joseph knew love. Joseph knew religious piety. Joseph knew social climate. Joseph needed God's Word to lift him above his limits.

The best place for doubt and uncertainty to thrive is on the edge of our personal limitations. They force us to centralize our thoughts, actions, and overall movement in life. When we move in life according to doubts, we find our purpose, hopes, dreams, and our destiny being imprisoned.

For Joseph, his marriage and happiness were being directly affected by doubt. What Joseph did not know before was that doubt was attempting to push him out of position to facilitate the safe arrival of salvation. Doubt was a pawn attempting to place redemption for humanity in checkmate. Only a word from God would change Joseph's perspective.

Many people know the feeling associated with limitations. Someone may tell you that your pursuit of education is unnecessary. Others have presented you with every reason why your business will fail. You have been bombarded by your past. Everything in your atmosphere has told you to stop dreaming, pursuing, and growing. Let me speak into your life. Don't listen!

Everything that God permits has an intended purpose. The setup for the deliverance was already documented in Genesis 3:15:

> *I will put enmity between you and the woman, and between your offspring and her offspring; he shall bruise your head, and you shall bruise his heel.*

The blueprint was set, but the details were never revealed until this particular moment with Joseph. God did not want Joseph to miss the significance of his place in the plan.

When we do not seek God to show us what to do in various moments of life, we subject ourselves to our reservoir of knowledge. We limit our opportunities by depending on other resources when God has the answers. We potentially forfeit our future without a word from God.

CLARITY RECEIVED

Joseph received a clear picture after God spoke. He saw where he fit in God's plan. Joseph recognized that Mary was still faithful, righteous, and committed as the day they met. Joseph saw the greater picture from this convoluted and confusing scene—salvation.

Paul writes a very appropriate phrase years later. *For now we see through a glass dimly*—this statement is buzzing with profound wisdom. The suggestion is that growth determines our level of clarity regarding the things of God. Simply put, nobody knows everything regarding the Creator.

Yes, we have built academic institutions dedicated to the pursuit of understanding the ins and outs of God. I have received three advanced degrees from two wonderful United Methodist schools. They fostered my intellectual rigor and challenged my theological proficiency. Yet, the classroom cannot teach or reveal the depths of God like personal relationship.

I am a supporter of going after higher education. My degrees and student loans tell that story. Education gives us tools and theories to exercise and see how we can effect positive change. However, it is never a substitute for engaging the Almighty.

Paul's image of a cloudy glass is a perfect analogy of how we pursue God. I grew up and still participate in the Baptist church tradition. Many people have their preconceived ideas about those from my background. It has annoyed me for so long that I usually don't talk about my denominational heritage. I talk Jesus. Why? Let me count the ways:

1. Presbyterian preschool
2. Nondenominational Christian school (K-3rd grade)
3. Nazarene Christian school (4th-10th grade)
4. Pastored two National Baptist churches
5. Grew up in a progressive National Baptist church
6. Served in two Missionary Baptist churches
7. Preached in a Disciples of Christ church for three years
8. Graduated from two UMC seminaries
9. Married a woman from a nondenominational background

I share this list for perspective. Nobody has a corner on the appropriate distribution of God. The church is a body of baptized believers in Jesus Christ. Furthermore, we are called to carry out the mandate of the Kingdom of God.

You noticed that last part of the previous paragraph? That phrase *Kingdom of God* has interpretations for many people. That term continues to cause fights among people daily. Yet, the idea has not made enough of us consider that our holy wars have not pushed us toward accomplishing God's purpose. No, sir and madam, we have created more darkness to justify not seeing God. In turn, we have declared our blindness as a condition caused by others and not of our own doing.

Let me step out and declare that clarity from God has the power to expose our deep-seated sexism, racism, classism, bigotry, and unnecessary bias. Joseph's original decision was affected by many of these issues. Yet, God refocused and redirected Joseph contrary to the norms of the day.

Here is a radical thought. Maybe it is time to do something different to see the Kingdom of God observed on earth. At this moment of your life, God might be trying to get you to see things differently.

The possibility exists that the assault on unarmed black men by authority figures is more than a wake-up call to protest for justice. It may also be a clarion call back to our heritage of loving community by investing in us. The call of *Black Lives Matter* becomes the rallying cry to get back to simple, God-led sacredness of humanity. The elections of Barack H. Obama and Donald J. Trump might be the triggers that uncovered vile hatred under the guise of post-racialism.

These thoughts and many others cannot be viewed through our cloudy prism. Otherwise, we will miss God in the details. Wisdom reminds us of this reality:

> *Trust in the* LORD *with all your heart, and do not lean on your own understanding. In all your ways acknowledge Him, and He will make straight your paths.*
> —Proverbs 3:5-6

A SOLID PROMISE

During this sequence, God gave Joseph a promise attached to this assignment. The promise was the ability to name salvation. *She will bear a son, and* you shall call his name Jesus, *for he will save his people from their sins* (emphasis added). Joseph was not the biological father. Joseph was not the originator of this manifestation of redemption. However, God made a promise to give Joseph authority and oversight over God's greatest gift.

Every once in a while, we need to step back and examine God's promises toward us. We might be figuratively placing emphasis on the wrong syllable. We seek the promises of God without considering the responsibility that comes with it. We want to be blessed, but we don't always want the responsibility.

Look at this again. God said that Joseph was important to the plan. He wanted Joseph to break away from the norms of the world. By doing this, Joseph would be able to name Jesus and claim the Savior as his own (much like adoption). Don't believe me? Read the whole story.

Joseph took Mary to Bethlehem because the Roman Empire was performing a census and kingdom taxation (Luke 2:1-4). When Jesus was in the temple showing off His understanding of God, Joseph looked for Him and received obedience and reverence from Jesus (Luke 2:41-52). Joseph was honored and blessed by God as the Creator promised.

My contention is that we have been seeking so many other gifts, blessings, and promises from God that we have missed the power of His *on the record* guarantees. Part of missing the guarantees is accepting the truth. We don't always want to work. We might not get it right. We are scared to fall on our faces.

God never asked us to master things on the first try. God just asked us to be willing. We must be taught. We must practice. We must grow. Yet, going forward by faith entitles us to access God's storage of blessings. Just look at a few.

> *Go therefore and make disciples....And behold, I am with you always, to the end of the age.*
> —Matthew 28:19-20

> *No weapon that is formed against you shall succeed... This is the heritage of the servants of the Lord...*
> —Isaiah 54:17

> *For all the promises of God find their Yes in Him. That is why it is through him that we utter our Amen to God for his glory.*
> —2 Corinthians 1:20

Never take for granted that God believes in you. Never take for granted that the Lord wants you to move beyond the box. God knows you are frightened today. God knows your challenges. The Lord just wants the chance to show you the bigger picture and guide you to your appointed place. Step beyond doubt into the sweet peace and relief of God's presence. Watch God work your destiny in your favor.

How are you doing over there? Has this trip been a little rough? Are you at least being encouraged at each phase? I really hope so. Not for my benefit, but I want you to know that this time in this valley, space is never wasted. I will admit that I should have probably informed you how close to the end you are.

Chapter 8

I Needed the Valley

> The Lord is my shepherd; I shall not want.
> He maketh me to lie down in green pastures:
> he leadeth me beside the still waters.
> He restoreth my soul:
> he leadeth me in the paths of righteousness
> for his name's sake.
> Yea, though I walk through the valley
> of the shadow of death,
> I will fear no evil: for thou art with me;
> thy rod and thy staff they comfort me.
> Thou preparest a table before me in the presence
> of mine enemies:
> thou anointest my head with oil; my cup runneth over.
> Surely goodness and mercy shall follow me
> all the days of my life:
> and I will dwell in the house of the Lord for ever.
> —Psalm 23, KJV

The end of a valley journey is full of emotions and entities attempting to convince you that this space is the final resting place for your existence.

Not so. Your journey continues beyond your doubts, fears, and past. Your life goes on beyond emotional, mental, and spiritual boundaries once set by previously acquired knowledge. God has worked out your inner difficulty in order for you to obtain your promise. It has been a useful experience, but it's not over.

Come on and take a seat by me at this table. We need to take a moment and really digest what we have experienced. Listen, I know you did not fully realize what to expect in this place. I tried my best to share with you what you may experience in the valley. So much is here that one trip does not cover everything.

This table conversation is to serve as a reminder that you are here to receive necessary tools and energy to go forward in life. You are here because of a myriad of possibilities. You didn't specify what brought you here, but I know it was not easy for you to come to this point. My prayer is that you laid down your pain, anger, disappointment, confusion, strife, and weariness. I pray that you have encountered the Good Shepherd.

Well, I can assume you did encounter the Lord here. The reason we are meeting at this table near your exit is because the Lord led you here. This place was made for you. We are here to celebrate that you have made it.

Being in the valley tests all of our emotions. Considering the reality of all types of past issues, failures, and other distractions lurking in the shadows, it is amazing how you turned out. You realize the challenge of your journey was to avoid being destroyed by the grips of your enemies. The isolation of this place normally makes us easy prey. However, the hand of the Lord has been upon you this entire time. Nobody is willing or able to confront the Lord and win.

This stop should place in you a new determination to press on in life. Since you are still here in this part of measured time, you have a purpose and destiny waiting for the stamp of fulfillment. The devil tried to cause failure to rise in your life. However, you are still here, still standing. You have a reason to enjoy this spread set by God.

Now allow me to be a better brother and share this truth with you. Even though the valley was not a vacation, it did represent a change from normal living patterns. It was an opportunity to reset and refocus our attention on what God wants and what we need beyond this place.

> **Since you are still here in this part of measured time, you have a purpose and destiny waiting for the stamp of fulfillment.**

Beyond this place...oh, you realize the world was still turning and preparing for your return. Oh, yeah! The enemy is upset you lasted so long here. Well, it's not the first time defeat happened in this setting. Jesus did set the precedent during His forty days away.

I mean Jesus was so slick the way that He handled the devil. Satan said, "You're hungry. Make some bread out of these rocks." Jesus replied, "I don't need anything but the Word" (Luke 4:1-4). Satan wanted Jesus to become a reality star through misappropriation of Scripture. Jesus didn't budge (vv. 9-12). I'm saying. How do you attempt to give someone his stuff like it is yours to give away (vv. 5-8)? Any encounter like that would make anyone jaded about desert or valley experiences.

We are a part of a group of overcomers that made it through the challenges, yet we must get ready for what is to come next. Many of these things have been discussed. However, I want to tell you the practical use of this educational trip for your next stage of life. Prayerfully, you have received restored confidence, a new assignment, and protection to continue traveling.

Confidence Restored

When you came to this valley patch, your confidence was tried. It happens to everyone. Job was confident in God's ability to keep him. Yet, Job became sick, children died, possessions lost, and relationships turned ugly. Samson was overconfident in his gift. God stripped him of everything, and Samson came in the valley a wounded man.

A prerequisite for entering this place is wounded confidence (or at least it appears that way). The journey gives us an accurate reading on where we source our confidence initially. Many of us began in the delusional place of being self-made, self-branded people. We leaned heavily on achievements, positions, education, material possessions, and pride only to have all of it poked, prodded, and ultimately dismissed.

Yes, we have the capacity to lose our minds. Yes, we have the ability to dismiss what matters. We do it when we believe we have arrived. God made all the difference in our lives, but we begin to believe our own hype.

Confidence is an important aspect of human life. The lack of confidence takes away from the boldness needed to confront challenges, opportunities, or the future. Confidence allows anyone to move toward being used effectively by God.

Remember David. He wrote Psalm 23 and countless others. We are currently sitting in his imagery. However, we must consider David's life for a moment. He was called *a man after God's own heart;* but he murdered, stole, and manipulated power. This reality does not exemplify the God I know.

However, David was known for his need to repent to God when he went astray. God never rejects genuine repentance. As a matter of fact, God will go extra steps in order to restore His people. Look at what David requested after messing up Bathsheba's life:

> *Create in me a clean heart, O God, and renew a right spirit within me. Cast me not away from your presence, and take not your Holy Spirit from me. Restore to me the joy of your salvation and uphold me with a willing spirit.*
>
> —Psalm 51:10-12

The source of David's confidence was rooted in his relationship with God. If that relationship was damaged, David did not stand a chance of making it further in life on his merit. David knew that he was in position as king because God deemed it so. David knew that as quickly as he obtained prominence, God could eliminate it.

When we are forgiven after genuine repentance, our confidence increases. Our confidence grows because we know our relationship with God is sure and solid. When Paul suggests that salvation is the helmet in our armor, do not overlook the significance.

Salvation marks you and me. Salvation always reminds us who we are and whose we are.

A New Assignment

Don't forget that when you leave here, you have a job waiting for you. This time was to repair and restore. Nevertheless, you have a new assignment on the horizon. You need to share your experience. When we leave this space, we are commissioned as Ambassadors of the Valley. The title is not CEO, but it is the right one.

Years ago, I learned how difficult it was to talk Bible when my life had never dealt with certain difficulties. Do not misunderstand me. I can articulate regarding most subject matter, but I had no *blood* on it. In other words, my experiences had not confronted normal growing moments. My articulation was wonderful oratory rooted in deep philosophical edification.

One trip to the valley changes our ability to sense and perceive God. We truly discover the meaning of *all things working together for our good.* We discover how important and necessary moments like these can be for us. Take an outcast woman's story as a resource.

An unnamed woman met Jesus at a well in the middle of the day. She was tired of being the subject of gossip and judgment regarding her multiple marriages and relationship of the moment. She has an encounter with Jesus and has a life-changing conversation about quality water, theology, and His messianic assignment.

Once she recognized that Jesus was not an average guy from the streets, the conversation moved her from public shame to willing herald. "Come see a man who told me all that I ever did. Can this be the Christ?" Her movement toward her new position of advertising compelled men and women to sit at the feet of Jesus.

May I reiterate that no one cares about the abundance of knowledge we may possess on a subject. People care if we are intimately involved with whom or what we know. People want to know that we possess conviction.

A steak that is cooked to perfection achieves that status when you eat it. Michael Jordan was clutch only when he hit game-winning shots. A preacher is compelling when he or she has been drawn in by God. A business owner is truly successful when he or she closes the deal. A new assignment is a sign of a new, deeper conviction in God.

Protection All Around

Before you leave, I want you to become familiar with your security detail—Goodness and Mercy. I want you to get to know them very well. They are fully acquainted with your destiny and purpose. The Lord designed them to be companions and preservers of the anointing on your life.

Realize that the oil placed on you is strong and attracts all types of traps and attacks. When you leave this valley, the price on your head will increase. The necessity to watch your downfall becomes a priority. God knows that. God recognizes that obstruction. It is for that reason the Holy Spirit must guide and comfort you internally. But, Goodness and Mercy will stand as tangible proxies along the way.

Let me tell you how good they are. When your bills are extremely high, your finances are nonexistent, but you call on the Lord, bills get paid, debts cancelled, and repositioning of your financial future unfolds. That activity is Goodness appealing to collectors and Mercy blocking deadlines.

No matter what the test, don't move without staying covered. We are not invincible. If we were untouchable, the need for God would be nonexistent. The valley would be a useless tool. Life would lack substance for the future. Never forget the guarantee attached to God's security.

> *He who dwells in the shelter of the Most High will abide under the shadow of the Almighty…*
> —Psalm 91

God promised to take care of us no matter the test. He promised to go before us and clear our path. The Lord does not fail to preserve us. We are not always fond of the methodology. Yet, God proves every time that the path we take is what is best for us. You are built up. Fired up. Now, let's see what awaits.

CHAPTER 9

JUST WHEN THEY SAID IT WAS OVER...

And he said to them, "What things?" And they said to him, "Concerning Jesus of Nazareth, a man who was a prophet mighty in deed and word before God and all the people, and how our chief priests and rulers delivered him up to be condemned to death, and crucified him. But we had hoped that he was the one to redeem Israel. Yes, and besides all this, it is now the third day since these things happened. Moreover, some women of our company amazed us. They were at the tomb early in the morning, and when they did not find his body, they came back saying that they had even seen a vision of angels, who said that he was alive. Some of those who were with us went to the tomb and found it just as the women had said, but him they did not see." And he said to them, "O foolish ones, and slow of heart to believe all that the prophets have spoken! Was it not necessary that the Christ should suffer these things and enter into his glory?" And beginning with Moses

and all the Prophets, he interpreted to them in all the Scriptures the things concerning himself.
—Luke 24:19-27

The valley journey has ended. It is time to return to the world. Whether you believe it or not, some people did miss your presence. When we reenter spaces that are common to us, it is understandable that these places do not always feel the same. Conversations are not the same. Interactions have lost some commonality. Your fit in those circles has become uncomfortable. The reason for that feeling—you are not the same.

You cannot go through a season of difficulty without being changed. Growth, challenge, and opposition grant us the blessing of expansion. Our thinking moves from limited to limitless. Our dreams expand from visions to tangible realities. Our resolve becomes strengthened by our experience.

All of these shifts in our lives unearth an unusual phenomenon that can be reduced to one question offered by our respective environments, *Why you being brand new?* This interrogative birthed out of colloquial English raises a peculiar idea. Your change is evident to everyone. Your renewal is not going to be accepted right away. Your changes are not going to be readily embraced. Understanding this reality is not difficult. The reasons behind this truth may shock you.

Everyone has a moment of growth and adjustment. That process is not the problem. Your growth does not match what has been said in your absence. That fact is the issue. Any time we walk away from the scene for a moment, room is made for opinion and conjecture about our departure.

Yes, our condition or status does not reduce the propensity for people to create strange and unusual ideas about us. But, the challenge of the detractors and gossipers is to figure out where their stories align with our different conditions. They cannot trace their assumptions with God's renewal.

When my family and I made the decision to leave Springfield, Illinois, the decision was not made in haste. The choice was never rooted in anger, disgust, or any other negative emotion. My wife was given an opportunity to grow and flourish in her career. That chance was granted in our hometown. Myrissa tried everything to apply for jobs all over Illinois.

No doors opened. We spoke about being in two different states for six months until my wife could go completely remote. However, a two-year-old boy did not want to be away from his daddy. As the priest of my home, I trusted God. It was the right decision.

How things were handled in the end could have had a better touch. Transition is never easy. So many people showed us love while we were in Springfield. Many people felt pain like we felt pain in moving. We still love the people to this day. Feelings can be complex when *suddenly* happens.

However, the assumptions and statements that some people made were loud, insulting, and cruel. Grown men questioned my manhood, saying I was following my wife. Church folk questioned my ministry calling. When I came back to Columbus, nosy preachers assumed I was kicked out of the church. Even a rumor was started that I quit preaching the Gospel altogether. Church folk said this stuff.

Even as I pen these thoughts, I think about the nights Myrissa watched me stew in anger and frustration. I remember her feeling no joy in her promotion due to the unkind and callous thoughts of fair-weather people. My heart could not take it. We were walking by faith knowing this adjustment was a God move, but believers decided to crucify our every move.

> **We must engage God to the extent that negativity must yield to the promise of God.**

I have attempted to truly understand this type of response to anyone trying to sincerely live for God. I still have not figured it out. Over thirty years of living has not given me a definitive, baseline answer. My limited knowledge informs me that human beings are flawed. People still function in default modes even when Jesus is on their minds.

We cannot change that thinking process of others. It is our responsibility to trust God in such a manner that entering into formerly, common locations will not become a deterrent but an opportunity. The goal is to walk so much in God that the environment has no alternative but to change. We must engage God to the extent that negativity must yield to the promise of God.

Furthermore, we must take a moment to recognize that the abundance of negative activity plays a role in our return. The vitriol provides a moment for God to show His will in the midst of opinions and opposing thought. God uses these platforms to prove to the cynic the yielding power of a Godly investment.

> *...so shall my word be that goes out from my mouth; it shall not return to me empty, but it shall accomplish that which I purpose, and shall succeed in the thing for which I sent it.*
>
> —Isaiah 55:11

On a path in the Jerusalem area, two men were having a discussion about the death of Jesus. They were trying to work through the crucifixion that stole their hope of a better future. They were also trying to address the message of Jesus' resurrection as delivered from the women who went to the tomb.

During this trek, Jesus joined the men. The twist of this walk was the men had no idea Jesus was walking with them. The men were asked about the nature of their lament. They looked at this stranger as if He had a second head growing out of the side of His neck. They could not believe that He did not know the breaking news of the day. Cleopas, one of the two travelers, opened up about the suffering and death of Jesus.

He expressed the greatness of all the deeds and miracles performed by Jesus. Cleopas reflected on the hope that was expressed through the teachings and ministry of Christ. He also addressed the reports of Christ's resurrection, but he had reservation about the story due to the lack of evidence. The promise of Jesus was not fulfilled because they had no tangibility.

When Jesus heard this emotional speech, He saw the right moment to interject the necessary peace to bring these heartbroken men back to a place of confidence in the message they first believed: "Was it not necessary that Christ should suffer these things and enter into His glory?" (Luke 24:26).

Jesus began offering an exegetical journey addressing the necessity for the bloody process of validating the heavenly message. The men were so engaged with the things spoken that they did not want the walk to end. They compelled Jesus to stay with them on the path they were taking.

Change and alternative results are tools to unearth a dormant purpose or promise.

Then, it happened. Jesus sat down with these traveling believers and began eating a meal. Jesus was given the privilege of breaking the bread. After the bread was broken, Jesus suddenly disappeared. The breaking of bread broke the curse of emotional blindness. They realized they were in the presence of the Risen Christ.

> *They said to each other, "Did not our hearts burn within us while he talked to us on the road, while he opened to us the Scriptures?"*
>
> —Luke 24:32

I can only imagine the looks on the faces of these men. Consider the manner they articulated the pain and suffering of what they witnessed three days prior. The visual evidence showed a beaten, bloodied leader. The evidence did not match the report of the women at the tomb.

Yet, Christ knew that every one of His followers needed a different encounter proving that His word and promise were fulfilled. These men saw Jesus before them. They heard the consistent message Jesus declared on many occasions. It was not until they witnessed a familiar sign that they recognized His presence (read Luke 22:14-20).

The change that happened with Jesus was opposed to the previous condition once witnessed. The response of the men may have been shock and awe, but it is common. Change and alternative results are tools to unearth a dormant purpose or promise. This challenge is necessary for a few reasons.

A Breeding Ground for Miracles

Take this image in for a moment. You see someone you place your hopes, dreams, and aspirations in, die before your eyes. You saw the blood. You saw the beating. You witnessed the agony. No doubt crosses your mind that this person has died. The scene was too graphic for you to forget anything.

Many people watched your suffering. Crowds gathered to experience your demise. People had meetings to discuss your former greatness. Enemies laughed at your gravesite. Observers tried to steal your legacy. You were good as gone. It was a public event.

> **Every time life devolves to its worse state, God uses the whole scene as an opportunity to demonstrate what a genuine miracle looks like.**

Every time life devolves to its worse state, God uses the whole scene as an opportunity to demonstrate what a genuine miracle looks like. Miracles come in all forms. However, all miracles do not make the same impact.

The woman with a blood condition met Jesus in the midst of a crowd. She was not welcomed in public, according to the law. She was unclean. She should not be among the crowd. Her condition was evident. However, her desire for change was greater.

The afflicted lady did not reach for the hem of the Master's garment to be seen. She reached for Him believing He could change her situation, whether He saw her or not. What is still strange about the story is Jesus decided to use the bleeding faith of an unclean woman to demonstrate that miracles do not happen because of clamoring or spatial proximity to the Savior. Unseen faith still moves God.

Even though our visual world may be suffering before people's eyes, it is not an indicator that God has ceased working within the heart and spirit of His child. I'm messed up today, but it won't last. My money is funny. Jobs will not say, *You're hired*. Yet, I will still trust in the plan of God! Say it with me: *I will rise from this place better than I began.*

Misplaced Expectations

One of the subtle things we forget about the perception of Jesus is that people were looking for an acute-moment Savior. Jesus came to save the world from their sins. However, many Israelites were not hoping for spiritual redemption. Political or military deliverance would have been enough.

Jesus performed signs, wonders, and miracles. He preached a message that granted the lowly and disenfranchised the hope of a better future. Everything about the ministry of Jesus over three years indicated a dynamic shift in culture, economics, government, and society.

When Jesus died, the instant hopes of a maligned people dissipated. They were tired of the Roman Empire. They could not stand the abuse of the Jewish religious hierarchy. The oppression was finally going to end, until Jesus died.

What these travelers discovered was the beauty of unsettled issues. Jesus rose from the dead to complete the plan of salvation. The Resurrection was also a signal to the world that His purpose was bigger than a moment. Jesus came to cover all of the ills of the world at the root. His appearing was the evidence that death could not win. The grave did not possess a grip to hold Him. Satan could not conquer. Jesus made the fiasco in the Garden a footnote rather than a demonic victory.

> **Our testimony must have the ability to speak to others about navigating through the peaks and valleys of life.**

People may examine our lives through limited views. Individuals have been critical because your greatness has not materialized in the time frame the world planned. Been there. Still facing it with you. But, our confidence must be expressed in a similar manner to Jesus:

> *I have said these things to you, that in me you may have peace. In the world you will have tribulation. But take heart; I have overcome the world.*
>
> —John 16:33

Our lives were not meant to be a collection of acute moments. Our collective purpose is not to fulfill short-term satisfaction. Our call to action is to endure the difficult moments. Our testimony must have the ability to speak to others about navigating through the peaks and valleys of life.

Unexpected Revelation

The end of the story has always been an amazing sign of the message of unity. Jesus broke bread with the travelers in the midst of fellowship. The moment was generated as the result of genuine pursuit of the presence of God and the unfiltered message of the Gospel. Consider the construction of this newly forged grouping. The gathering was built on three elements: the blood, the Word, and communion. Sounds like *church* to me.

This revelation serves as a reminder to us all. When we emerge from our experience with the Lord, our biggest discovery is who will sit at this new table. This spread is not reserved for a single seat. God created this space for all who will embrace the Word, the presence of God, and communion with brothers and sisters in the faith.

I am convinced that a greater blessing comes from going through the valley than change alone. God allows us the time to go away from view so that we might rid ourselves of unhealthy relationships, opinions, and perspectives. No longer bound by the weight of oppressive thoughts, we are able to embrace new opportunities for growth, fellowship, and unity.

Our circles may never be the same. Supporters may become doubters. Leeches will grow into stepping-stones. Rivals may become your greatest advocates. No matter the shift, your table is set for those who will bind themselves to the Gospel that holds you.

Therefore, I finish with this thought: Smile. Your process has not failed. It has enhanced you. The journey has ended at this stage, but your growth continues. Do not stop at this moment and believe you will never return to the valley. You will.

> **Remember, you cannot encounter God in any stage of life without being made new.**

Know this. The next visit may be very different. The purpose for your return may be distinct from this entry. But, take these lessons and thoughts as a foundation for understanding. Remember, you cannot encounter God in any stage of life without being made new. Welcome back. The Kingdom needs you. The world is waiting on you.

Final Thought

Uncovering

A few years ago, I wrote a piece that reflected a very difficult moment in my life. Strangely enough, this piece still has great relevance to my journey. I believe it is important to never forget the valley moments that shape your present and future. I also believe that you should not be ashamed to tell your testimony, especially when you have passed the test.

I realize that you may not be the most profound speaker, extroverted personality, or open walking book. Let me encourage you that your journey, victory, challenges, and experience are important to the benefit and growth of the Kingdom of God. Your victory is not just for you. It is for us. My victories are not just for me. They are for you. Be empowered to go forward. Peace.

I have dealt with a wide range of emotions over the past few weeks. I must admit that trying to be introspective can be very difficult at times. Most people that attempt to tell you that they know all about you have very poor insight into who you are and what you are all about. Even more people attempt to define your purpose in this life according to unfavorable encounters with your purpose. I have learned in my short time on this earth that it is important not to define for people who I am, but give insight into the person I am becoming. *Well, why in the world would you do that?* I'm glad you asked. I believe that I have a responsibility to give people some understanding about my motivation for serving God the way I do.

Let me say that I am unapologetic about being a mouthpiece for God. I know that I am not worthy of being a pastor. I am not worthy by my merit of being blessed by the Lord. However, I am grateful that the Lord decided to use me anyway. I realize that many times I will not be the most popular person in the room. I am called to preach and teach a Gospel that is not popular with people that are content with status quo living, average views of life, and the lack of vision and purpose. I know that people will be constantly offended because of what the Gospel has to say.

Nevertheless, I have good news for all who feel offended by various messages from the Gospel. We who follow Jesus Christ have been offended. It was offensive to find that my life outside of Christ was crap. It was offensive to discover that all people who continued to hold me down were demonic forces in my life. It was offensive to realize that I devalued my life so much that at one point I was willing to play God and try to take my life. That's right! Suicidal thoughts permeated my mind because of demonic bullies, painful fatherless realities, and the lack of finding my place as an individual. The offensive Gospel caused me to realize that my crappy existence did not have to continue.

Since I discovered how powerful my God truly is, my life has never been the same. You see, I still remember the day that I tried to end my life at the age of twelve. I remember the moments that everyone called me fat, ugly, worthless, etc. I remember how I was called soft for crying real tears. I remember being called gay because I chose (and struggled) to be a virgin. I remember females telling me that I was not good enough. I remember being ostracized for living for Christ. I remember being told I was not smart enough to succeed. I remember all these things.

> **God is looking for His people to be strong enough to tell the truth and allow the truth to strengthen and empower us.**

I realize that if the Lord had not picked me up out of my depression, heartache, heartbreak, and disappointment, I would not be in this world today. I would have never attempted to pursue my purpose in this world. Because of the demonstration of love, I know that God truly cares about me and everything He invested in me.

My personal drive in life and ministry is to never miss an opportunity to tell someone that life is more than the ups and downs that come. One's life is more valuable in the hands of God than subject to the will of people that do not care. God is looking for His people to be strong enough to tell the truth and allow the truth to strengthen and empower us.

I pray that I never become the type of person that forgets my past. I pray that I will continue to be driven by God to illuminate the path of wholeness to those who need it most. I decided to share this portion of my life to let someone know that God can do anything and everything for you when you trust and believe in Him. Nothing in this world can keep you from being you if you are in the hands of God. My prayer is that this testimony and insight will serve as a moment of encouragement. You can uncover your wounds, pain, and suffering of your past. Know that God is ready, willing, and able to heal and deliver you from tragedy to triumph! God bless you.

About the Author

A native of Columbus, OH, Dr. C. Walter Ferguson has dedicated his life to the preaching and teaching of the Gospel. For the past twenty years, Dr. Ferguson has been involved in various pastoral and ministry assignments focusing on equipping, empowering, and educating believers on being Kingdom citizens. He has demonstrated the importance of education in his journey, graduating from Kentucky

State University (BA, Business Administration), Methodist Theological School in Ohio (MDiv and MA, Counseling Ministries), United Theological Seminary (DMin, Prophetic Preaching and Effective Church Leadership in the Twenty-first Century). He has been honored by both of the seminaries that he has attended with the distinction of being the first Charles E. Booth Preaching Conference Scholar (United) and the Baccalaureate Preacher (Methodist Theological) for his 2010 graduating class. The best part of his life is being husband to his wife, Myrissa, and father to his son, Charles Jeremiah.

www.ingramcontent.com/pod-product-compliance
Lightning Source LLC
LaVergne TN
LVHW051523070426
835507LV00023B/3276